THINGS THAT GO BUMP IN THE FLIGHT

A Whiteknuckler's Guide to Air Travel

Capt. Robert Welch

BETTERWAY PUBLICATIONS, INC.
White Hall, Virginia

Published by Betterway Publications, Inc.
Box 75
White Hall, Virginia 22987

Typography by Typecasting

Library of Congress Cataloging in Publication Data

Welch, Robert, 1932–
    Things that go bump in the flight

      1. Air Travel. 2. Aeronautics — Safety measures.
I. Title.
HE9787.W45   1987   629.13′0028   87–1418
    ISBN 0-932620-75-2 (pbk.)

Printed in the United States of America
0 9 8 7 6 5 4 3 2 1

To my wife, Lyn

CONTENTS

It must be understood from the beginning that this book will never enter anyone's archives as a monument of literary achievement. Those that seek beautifully crafted phrases dealing with the world aloft have already found the works of Ernest Gann and Richard Bach. I envy the skills of these gentlemen.

This book is not about the glory of flight, as thousands of airmen view it, but is directed toward the occasional passenger who sees little or no glory in air travel and regards flying with a considerable measure of distaste. There is little likelihood that these words of mine will make anyone love flying because, for most, flying from city to city is only an alternative to spending hours on a crowded highway. Flying is the way a person can move about the country efficiently, and that is all it will ever be. Far too many people approach flying with nerve endings at full quiver. They do not take to the air very often and can't be expected to understand everything that is going on around them.

Therefore, we will answer some of the questions that almost every inexperienced traveler has wanted to ask, but didn't know where to find the answers. We will take a routine flight and describe what is going on. Then we will get a little abnormal. Then a lot abnormal. You will meet the crews and their machines. You will see the strengths and the weaknesses of the safest means of travel ever devised by man, learn how it got that way and how it stays that way. We will describe the flaws in the system, trying all the while to keep these flaws in perspective.

We will not be giving inside hints on how to obtain the cheapest possible ticket. The bushes are full of travel agents who can accommodate you in this manner; however, you may also choose to put those low fares in perspective when you select your airline. Remember, in air travel as in everything else, "You always get what you pay for."

If, by giving you some honest exposure to the world of airline flying, even to the point of thundering boredom (as may well be the case in the Airplane chapter) we may be able to put to rest some of the fables and myths that have caused you some anxiety.

We will not be spending a lot of time with statistics. This juggling of numbers is very comforting to those who spend their lives developing the Big Picture, so that everything works out mathematically. We can give this same person a neatly typed set of statistics dealing with how safe he is on an airplane, then put him on board an airliner in the middle of an old fashioned New England snowstorm. Chances are that he will take those neatly logical numbers and fold them up to serve as a doily for the double martini he will order before takeoff.

Genuine fear of flying is very real to those who suffer it. To some professionals who must travel a great deal, it can be crippling to their careers. Those who must force themselves to fly, and hate every minute of the ordeal, cannot be as effective in their work as they could be if they were able to accept flying as simply another tool of their business lives.

A family, on vacation and unable to fly, is going to spend a great deal of that vacation on the highways. Not a very relaxing way to relax.

I, along with whole regiments of airline marketing types, wish we had answers for those who simply can't calm their jitters long enough to give airline flying a try. Neither I, nor they, have any magic at our disposal to brush away deep-seated fears. That takes another kind of professional.

The airlines want these people to fly for the obvious reason, profit. However, I have a more personal reason for wanting to break through those walls of trepidation. Like most pilots, I work hard at making every flight as safe and comfortable as I possibly can. I thoroughly enjoy it when my passengers stop by the cockpit after landing to say that they enjoyed the flight. It means that I am doing my job well. I try to fly each flight as if the passenger list were comprised solely of "White Knucklers," because each flight will have at least one such a person aboard. If we are going to be near a thunderstorm, with a lot of flashy lightning, I try to tell them not to worry. I like to keep my passengers informed of anything that they might regard as threatening.

If, with my humble efforts, I can explain the things you don't need to fear and put some of your fears to rest, then you and I will have accomplished something of value.

You have gotten your ticket and now you are at the gate. Now it is time to fly, so read on and maybe you and I can take a little of the dread out of your flight.

No surprises.

That is the real purpose of this book. No surprises. So let's get on with it.

From ghoulies and ghosties
And long legged beasties
And things that go bump in the night,
Good Lord, deliver us.

— Scottish prayer

CHAPTER 1

INTO THE DEEP END... HEAD FIRST

Let's start by taking a flight from La Guardia airport in New York to the Atlanta airport, where you can make connections to almost anywhere in the country. A few years ago, before their new terminal complex was completed, the Hartsfield airport in Atlanta gained quite a reputation for being...well, inefficient. The word was that on the day one passed away, WHETHER bound for Heaven or Hell, the soul must first pass through Atlanta. There the soul would have to wait for a gate, miss its connection and lose its baggage. (Hence the dictum, "you can't take it with you, 'cause it'll never get through Atlanta.")

However, the new terminal in Atlanta has made life much easier for the connecting traveler, so we will route you through there.

Our flight will be uneventful, as almost every flight you will ever take will be. No drama, no thrills...just an efficient way to get from New York to Atlanta in only a few hours. A little later, we'll toss in a few abnormalities that you could, one day, encounter. But for now, it will be just a routine trip.

RULES TO REMEMBER BEFORE THE FLIGHT

I promise to make your flight a bit more pleasant, but you can do a lot in that direction before you even leave your home or office.

RULE 1. Pack light. If you don't need it, leave it home. If you are packing for a vacation, put as much as you can in one large bag, and take only what you will need for the flight in a smaller, carry-on type bag. If you are traveling on one of the new, "deregulation" airlines, the ones with the bargain basement fares, this is doubly important. You will be your own baggage handler in this case, even up to the point of paying extra for the privilege of loading your own bags into the baggage compartment of the airplane, and retrieving them at the end of the trip, with no connecting service to any other airline. If you are taking special medication, get one of those little pill boxes and keep the medicine on your person in a pocket, not a purse.

RULE 2. Get to the airport early. O.J. Simpson made a lot of money by running through airports — you will not. All you will get is a coronary, lousy seat assignments and/or a few missed flights. Check in with the ticket counter early, and you will get a much better selection of seats and run little chance of being "bumped" in the event that the flight is overbooked. Overbooking results from "no shows." A businessman's secretary will reserve space on several flights, and then the boss can take the one that best fits his fluid schedule. The other reservations are not cancelled, and the airline ends up with a lot of empty seats when the flight actually leaves. To try to protect themselves, the airlines accept more reservations than there are seats on the flight. Usually, the overbookings are balanced out by the "no shows," and the flight departs with only a few empty seats.

That's the way it works until *you* show up late, and everyone else got there early, and there you stand...watching your flight depart with a confirmed reservation in your outraged hand. You should try very hard to arrive at the boarding gate at least 30 minutes before departure time. At about 10 minutes before departure, the gate agents will begin calling "standby passengers" and board them. Once a standby passenger has taken a seat on the airplane, the agents will probably not ask him or her to leave the aircraft to accommodate you, should you show up at the last minute. The agents are trying to get the flight out as nearly on time as possible. If your flight has been delayed, don't wander off to the nearest bar and wait till the last minute to pay your tab and return to the gate. Very few airport public address systems operate in the bars and restaurants, so you will not receive warning of your flight's departure. Follow these two rules and your day will go much smoother.

BOARDING TIME

Often the gate area will have windows where you can watch your airplane being serviced. A long tunnel leads to the ship, and trucks of every conceivable size and shape surround it.

Catering trucks with bodies that rise to the galley door of any size airplane, bringing food and drink for the expected number of passengers; fuel trucks pump thousands of pounds of highly refined kerosene aboard; and large, truck-mounted conveyer belts assist in the loading of freight and baggage; a few mechanics' vans join in the general clutter.

The poor old airplane itself looks untidy with flaps and panels drooping and sagging. Once the engines are started and hydraulic power is available, these panels will move to their proper places. We will have a closer look at these flaps a little later, but now it's time to board.

As you line up in the "jetway," the long loading bridge to the airplane, you feel the floor beneath you suddenly drop a bit. Explanation: as the aircraft pulled up to the gate, it was light on fuel and heavy with passengers. The passengers began to file off and the airplane began to rise, now relatively unburdened by either fuel or passengers. There is a hydraulic system installed on the jetway that can jack up, or lower, the whole bridge assembly keeping the floor of the bridge level with the floor of the airplane. A sensor resting against the skin of the airplane signals the hydraulics to go up or down with the movement of the plane. While you were boarding, fuel and freight were also being loaded and the airplane began to settle on its shock absorbers. "Bump," the jetway drops to match it. You have just had your first "Bump in the Flight," and you are not even aboard yet.

You are going to be boarding a Boeing 727, not the newest or fanciest bird in the skies, but one of the most reliable and typical of almost every jetliner manufactured over the last 25 years. There are also more 727s than any other type (over 1800 built) so the odds are great that you will fly on one of these fine aircraft.

On a recent vacation, I visited the Boeing factory in Seattle, Washington, and witnessed the last 727 to ever be built, on the assembly line. Two weeks later, I flew aircraft N8101E, the first 727 to be built — ship 101. Old, but proud, she still handles as well as a brand new one. Sadly, the last 727 to be delivered was destined to be a freighter.

Once on board, find your seat and stow your carry-on baggage beneath the seat in front of you or in the enclosed overhead bin, then relax. If you are traveling in the coach section, and you checked in early enough, you will instantly

✈

see the virtue of that early check-in. You probably have either a window or aisle seat, with a little more room than the person who got the center seat. No center seat can comfortably accommodate anyone who is equipped with arms and legs and is over the age of 12. If fate does seat you in one of these "restraints," spend the whole of your flight promising yourself that no force will ever again prevent you from arriving early, early, early for a flight.

TRAVEL LIGHT

You will also observe the reason for my advice to "travel light." The great American public has some sort of natural reluctance to ever leave anything at home. Tennis rackets, ski poles, television sets and large tropical plants are but a few of the things that ". . . brand X let me bring on board, last week." In fact, brand X is under the same federal law that restricts carry on articles to those that will fit in the prescribed areas. Don't try to con the flight attendants into allowing you to bring your "priceless van Gogh" on board. (You send a van Gogh home in a Brinks truck, not under the seat of an airliner.) The cabin attendants have heard every single reason conceived for bringing outsized articles onto airplanes, and rejected them all. They have all heard tales of trying to evacuate an airplane while people try to climb over great piles of debris. If you were to get abusive, and mention your personal relationship with the president of the line, the Captain will usually offer you a quarter and invite you to call your friend. . . now, while he leaves without you. As mentioned above, this federal ruling is designed to insure that the aisles will remain clear of carry-on luggage, should it ever be necessary to leave the airplane in a hurry.

CARRY-ON RESTRICTIONS

Another rule that bears mentioning is the matter of electronic devices and their use in the cabin. Most airlines have approved the use of small, portable computers in flight (check this out with the individual airline) as well as Dictaphones or any tape playback machines. The "Walkman" tape players are fine as well as the "boom boxes," and most airlines welcome them as long as the listener uses the headphones and does not disturb others. A little Beethoven helps to pass the hours on a long flight. However there is one real no-no. FM and television receivers cannot be operated during flight. The reason for this rule is that even receivers emit some radiation when operated in the FM band. If the user is seated near one of the navigation antennas (located directly on the top and bottom of the aircraft), these radiations can, and have, affected the navigation instruments. This effect is especially true during the most critical phase of flight—the instrument approach—since the instrument landing system radio frequencies are very near those of the FM radio band. As ever, whatever you bring onboard must fit beneath the seat or in some other approved area.

This carry-on problem is the single largest area of concern that the flight attendants must deal with each day. These are not airline rules but federal law. Flight crew members are reluctant to fool around with federal laws.

SECURITY SEARCHES

Earlier, I mentioned the subject of being abusive. At this point, let me give you a few hints on how to complete your flight as planned and stay out of jail. Obviously, you should not attempt to carry any kind of weapon onboard an airliner, and that includes anything more threatening than a fingernail clipper. Security procedures are getting very sophisticated and successful. Last year, more than 2000 potential weapons were confiscated at security check points. These weapons included hand guns, knives and, incredibly, machine guns and hand grenades. Many of these were replicas or non-operational weapons, but they are still unwelcome on an airliner.

In that same vein, once you reach security, forget that you ever heard the words, "Hijack," "Bomb," or any other phrases that might even be mistaken for these terms. Do not joke about it, or even whisper about it. If you were to spot your friend, Jack Spratt, strolling through the terminal, don't shout "Hi Jack." This may seem excessive; however, the terrorists of the world are starting to play hardball and so are the people who must protect you.

If you are the kind of person who feels that your rights are being infringed upon with security searches, stay out of airports...period. These things are taken very, very seriously. If you don't want to believe me, you might want to check with a certain ex-senator who refused to go through the screening process and was refused boarding by the captains of two separate airlines. (At the time, the gentleman was the senator from Indiana, and he regarded his civil rights as under attack. Actually, one suspects that the good senator regarded himself as being above such practices that were designed for the "commoner elements." He finally gained passage on a third airline, several hours later — after being searched.)

GETTING READY FOR DEPARTURE

Cute comments as you board the airplane, such as, "I hope you guys were not out drinking all night," or, "Think you can get this death trap off the ground?" are decidedly unwelcome. You may be joking, but the passenger behind you in line may not know that. Get too smart, and you may very well find yourself waiting for the next flight...or down at the bus station. If you were so foolish as to start kidding around about bombs or hijackings onboard, and a crew member overheard you, then I promise that the next few hours of your life will be unpleasant in the extreme, and the misery may not stop in just a few hours. I repeat, don't do it. I, personally, have never made a "side trip," but I have landed with a reported bomb aboard. I do not regard it as a joking matter.

Do not try to drink liquor from your own carry-on flask. It is against federal law and you jeopardize the license of the captain and expose the airline to a large fine if you do. I was recently forced to deplane half a dozen football fans who refused to stop drinking from their own bottles and were getting abusive with the cabin crew.

Okay, that's enough of the "don'ts." Let's get on with the flight itself.

Shortly before departure, you may notice a flicker in the lights. The flight engineer has just switched the airplane's electrical system from the external, or ground, power to the airplane's own, onboard, auxiliary power unit. This APU, as it is called, provides not only electrical energy for the ship until the engines are started, but compressed air for air conditioning and for starting the engines. I am trying to stay relatively non-technical for now, but we will be talking about the electrical system and all the other systems of the airplane a bit later in the book.

The airflow through the air conditioning system stops, and it is time to start the engines. The poor little APU cannot operate the air conditioning system and start the engines at the same time.

As the engines start, the lights may flicker once more. The electrical system has now shifted to the engine-driven generators.

The actual departure from the gate will vary at different airports with different airplanes. Here at La Guardia, a powerful tractor will push us away from the gate. At other airports you may experience a "power back," during which the engines are put in "reverse thrust" and the airplane backs away from the gate on its own power — quite noisy, but effective and faster than the tractor. Disconnected from the tractor, we are now ready to taxi to the runway.

TAXI TO THE RUNWAY

Now is as good a time as any to discuss the term "taxi." We taxi from the terminal to the runway and, after landing, back again. Any ground movement of the airplane is to "taxi" it. There are certain things in life that we must simply accept on faith, and I have no clue as to why one "taxis" an airplane instead of "drive" it. On my very first training flight as a brand new cadet, my instructor, with a nervous tremor in his voice, suggested that I taxi out to the runway. Since anything an instructor suggests to a new cadet carries the weight of having been chiseled in stone, I voiced no objection and released the brakes. The machine, once safely stationary, immediately turned around in a tight circle known as a "ground loop," which is not to be confused with orderly movement on the ground. I have found no reason to question this terminology, and on my last flight of this life, I will reluctantly taxi from the runway to the terminal.

On the subject of terminology, the question may arise as to why pilots call their work place a "cockpit." Again I must confess no knowledge of the origin of the term. Here, though, we have seen attempts to revise the cockpit into something else. "Control Cabin" and "Flight Deck" are but two attempts to alter the way people think of the place where pilots work. I suspect that some pitifully small person saw some vague sexual overtone in the name and decided to "de-odorize" it. To this I say, "PIFFLE!" The ancient Egyptians had a term, "MA-AT," which meant that there is a correct and proper way that things are, have always been and forever will be. So it is with cockpits.

As the airplane taxis out, the flight attendants are giving their safety demonstrations concerning emergency exits, life vests and such. To a very large degree they could save their breath. For varied reasons, few people pay much attention to these announcements and even those who do listen intently get very little of value from them. A principal reason for this inattention is that airlines are very reluctant to even mention the possibility that anything could go wrong on one of their flights. Therefore they clean up these federally required "demos" until they are, for the most part, useless. Crewmembers pray that if they ever do encounter a problem, it will be one in which there is time to give a real, detailed briefing. We will be devoting an entire chapter of this book to potential emergencies and what you can do to help yourself.

THE PILOT TESTS THE FLIGHT CONTROLS

Meanwhile, relax and watch the light snow swirl past your window—not a real blizzard but just a soft flurry. The skyline of Manhattan is still softly visible and the tugs in the East River are still pulling New York's garbage out to the sea in great barges. La Guardia itself is built on the refuse of another generation of New Yorkers...and is slowly sinking into the East River—but not today.

While you are gazing out of the window, you hear the whine of a motor, and watch the wing start to come apart. Large panels on the rear of the wing begin to droop and the front of the wing seems to be going all to pieces. The flaps are being lowered for takeoff. At the same time, smaller panels on top of the wing pop up and then return to their "faired" position. This latter movement is a result of the pilot's testing of the flight controls.

The wing flaps "reshape" the wing, making it aerodynamically "fatter," so that our 150,000 pound airplane will be able to take off from the relatively short runways of La Guardia. With flaps down, we can lift off at about 138 knots, and use only about 3500 feet of runway. Without these wingflaps, we would require all of the runway, and almost 210 knots to leave La Guardia. Chances are we would end up bobbing about in the river, halfway to Riker's Island. These flaps simply fool the airplane into thinking it has a slow speed, high-lift wing. Once airborne, and having accelerated to higher speeds, we can retract the flaps in stages, and reshape the wing, once again, for high speed flight.

"FLIGHT ATTENDANTS, PLEASE TAKE YOUR POSITIONS FOR TAKEOFF." This announcement, from the cockpit, says that we have been cleared onto the runway and will depart soon. If you are a confirmed "white knuckler," now is the time for you to do your thing, if it makes you feel any better.

TAKEOFF

The takeoff is regarded by some as the most critical part of any flight and is accorded a great deal of attention. One does not simply line up with the runway, wind up the engines and hope for the best.

Briefly, the standard that any airplane must meet before it can carry passengers states that: "Fully laden, the aircraft must demonstrate its ability to accelerate to a predetermined 'safety speed,' experience a failure of the aircraft's most critical engine, and be brought to a complete halt within 80% of a wet runway. If there is insufficient runway to meet this criterion, with the aircraft at maximum weight, then the weight of the aircraft is reduced until the standard can be met." That "safety speed" is called "V-1," and is regarded as a "go–no go" speed. "V-R" (rotation speed) comes soon after, and is the speed at which the pilot raises the nose to give the wings the proper angle to fly. Finally, "V-2" speed is reached, almost instantly after "V-R," and the airplane is assured the ability to continue its climb over any obstacle in its path, still assuming an engine failure.

So, as you can see, the takeoff is carefully calculated. About the best thing that can be said about it is that it works great, every time.

There is little doubt when the takeoff begins. The engines increase in power until they almost seem to be gnawing at the air and you are pressed gently back in your seat. You feel a bit of swaying from side to side as the pilot maintains the center line of the runway, and the concrete surface is beginning to rush past at a rapidly increasing rate. You may feel an occasional "thump, thump, thump" as the nose wheel passes over some runway lights that mark the center of the strip.

"V-1...ROTATE" The airplane is now committed to

flight, since the ability to abort the takeoff has just hurtled past at about 140 knots. The nose of the airplane rises to about a 10° angle, a few last rattles and bumps from the wheels and a tentative, soft smoothness...you are flying.

The snow streaks by your window, barely visible, and you hear a sudden rush of air. A few seconds pass and you can feel a few distinct "thumps," then the rushing sound disappears. Large doors on the belly of the airplane have opened, the landing gear has folded into the belly, and the doors have closed, streamlining the craft. Often you will feel, more than hear, a vibration as the nose wheel spins down in its compartment. This vibration decreases rapidly in frequency and is soon gone. Braking action has been applied to the main landing gear wheels before they were retracted.

CLIMBING TO HIGHER ALTITUDES

Briefly, as you continue your climb, you can watch the prison at Rikers Island slide off the right side of the plane, and the whitewashed ghost of Manhattan fades from view on the left. Now mist streams over the wing and you are in the clouds...a little like being in a swirling bottle of milk. A few mild bumps, and you notice that the panels on the top of the wing seem to float, randomly up and down. Look a little more closely and you will see two flaps which, until now, have been streamlined on the trailing edge of the wing. These flaps are moving slightly up and down. These panels did not droop down with the flaps and are solely for control of the airplane. If you could watch both wings at the same time, you would notice that as these panels moved up on one wing, they would go down on the other, forcing the airplane into or out of a turn, or "bank."

The upper panels are known as "spoilers" since they spoil the shape of the wing, and reduce lift, ever so slightly. The trailing edge controls are called ailerons. On our Boeing 727, there are two such devices on each wing. A small aileron is located at about the mid point of the wing, and operates all the time. A larger unit is further out, toward the end of the wing. This aileron only operates when the trailing edge flaps are extended for takeoff or landing, providing more control at the lower climb and approach speeds, and is not needed at very high speeds.

Shortly after takeoff, you were able to watch the wing

flaps retract into the trailing edge of the wing surface in short stages. Airborne, the airplane accelerates very rapidly and the wing no longer needs to be quite as "fat" to provide the same amount of lift. By the time we reach about 215 knots, the wing is "clean" (the flaps are fully retracted) and we can get serious about going fast. First, though, we must climb above 10,000 feet of altitude, since there is a "speed limit" of 250 knots below that altitude. This speed limit is imposed on jets because most small, private airplanes fly below 10,000 feet. We climb rapidly at the lower speed, getting out of the lower, crowded airspace quickly. Then, above 10,000 feet, we can pick up our speed to "cruise climb" velocities, usually between 300 and 320 knots.

WHAT IS A KNOT?

KNOTS, KNOTS, KNOTS. What is this man talking about? What is wrong with using good, old-fashioned, all-American miles per hour?

The world is divided up into degrees of latitude (around) and longitude (pole to pole). Each degree, as depicted on navigational maps, equals 60 nautical miles — an even division of distance. Since jets use these maps and fly to points that are designated in degrees of latitude and longitude, it is only logical that we use nautical miles per hour to calculate speed, flying time and so on. The speedometer in your car is calibrated in statute miles per hour, and a statute mile is shorter than a nautical mile. (One nautical mile is equal to 1.1507794 statute miles.) The term "knot" means nautical mile.

Let's stay with the subject of speed, while we climb out through the clouds. There is not a whole lot to see out the window, anyway.

Pilots are often asked, "How fast were we going?" Often, the pilot will pull a number out of the air that would roughly approximate statute miles per hour, simply because it sounds faster, and everybody wants to think that they are zipping right along. Actually, he could give you five answers, and all of them would be correct. The "air speed indicator" (speedometer) reads the air that flows over the airplane and is not corrected for temperature or the fact that the air is less dense at altitudes above sea level. (As altitude increases, air pressure de reases. The air thins out.) He needs this information to insure that sufficient air density is passing over his wing to provide lift. However, this does not tell him how fast he is traveling over the ground at the higher altitudes, and he needs this for navigation. A computer senses the temperature and the altitude and comes up with a corrected or "true air speed." The uncorrected speed is "indicated airspeed." At 35,000 feet altitude, for example, the airspeed indicator would read about 260 knots while the true airspeed would be approximately 425 knots. So, that is how fast we are traveling over the ground, right? Wrong. At least, hardly ever.

The wind is almost always blowing at the upper altitudes and, naturally, it affects how fast the machine is actually going to get from point "A" to point "B." A "head wind," one that is blowing opposite to your direction of flight, is going to slow you down, while a tail wind will help you along. This speed, true airspeed corrected for winds, is known as "ground speed"— how fast you are really covering the distance between any two points. Wind velocities of up to 180 knots are common at high altitudes.

Those are three speeds you deal with in high altitude flight, but there is a fourth...Mach. The speed of sound is referred to as Mach 1, and below that is sub-sonic speed. There is, just below Mach 1, a region called trans-sonic, which is a transition speed during which parts of the airplane actually come very close to being supersonic. It is in this region that the airplane is designed to fly—at least we used to fly in this region. The airlines once happily bored holes in the sky at Mach .84, or 84% of the speed of sound, but then, certain Middle Eastern nations learned of the value of oil and the price started going up...and the speeds started coming down. The difference in fuel consumption between Mach .84 and Mach .78 is dramatic, so that's where most airplanes cruise.

The fifth speed is the rough conversion from nautical to statute miles per hour, for those passengers who want to think that they have been going lickety-split. 425 knots equals 490 statute miles per hour. Statute Miles Per Hour simply sounds faster, but has no practical value to the pilot.

HOW ABOUT A COCKTAIL?

Enough of speeds. A flight attendant has just offered you a cocktail, and you go for a scotch. O.K., but go easy. Unless you are used to drinking in Denver, you can get pickled in a hurry. The altitude in the cabin, as the airplane nears its cruise altitude, is still at about 6000 feet. Perfectly safe, but the lowered oxygen content of the air gives booze an extra kick. The eyes glaze quickly and one tends to fall in love rapidly, with anyone who is nearby. Never propose marriage to anyone you met on an airplane—at least until you get to know that person on the ground.

KEEP YOUR SEAT BELT FASTENED

The captain comes on the P.A. and announces that he is turning off the seat belt sign and asks that you keep your seat belt fastened while you are seated. Sounds a little silly. Why turn off the sign if he still wants you strapped in? Federal law requires that a crew member make this announcement any time that the seat belt sign is off. More important, common sense dictates that you follow his advice. Move around the cabin if you like but, while seated, it doesn't cost a penny to have your seat belt loosely fastened.

Pilots will work very hard to avoid turbulence, but every once in a great while, one blunders into what is called CAT ...Clear Air Turbulence. There is no way to forecast it; it does not show up on any radar and is not predictable. Usually, CAT is in the form of light, choppy air. But, on rare occasions, it can give you a real thrill ride. A few people have been hurt by bouncing around the cabin, unrestrained. Believe the man; stay buckled up.

ENCOUNTERING A THUNDERSTORM

You break out of the clouds near Winchester, Virginia, and continue to climb into the dusk. Off to the west, the sun has settled below a thick wall of thunderstorms, standing like warriors with pointed caps. Their bodies pulse with blue-white lightning and the peach flame sky gives the impression of a battle, fully joined. There is no sight in the airman's world that can stir such silent gratitude as the view of a towering squall line when said airman knows that the line will not be within 100 miles of his route. The emotion is quite different when the storm is viewed out the front windshield.

One man who feared thunderstorms above all things on earth, or the heavens above, was Captain C. Having been in a few storms, during his career as a co-pilot, before the days of radar, C had learned that man's proper place in space was anywhere that thunderstorms were not.

The DC-7 had been droning northbound to Chicago, late one evening, with C relaxing while his co-pilot flew the bird. Misty clouds had enshrouded them for the last hour, but the flight had been smooth and C decided to get on the public address system and chat with the passengers. He was well into this talk, soothing his flock and speaking of the nice weather that awaited them in the Windy City, when the co-pilot thought he saw what could have been a flash of lightning somewhere far ahead. The co-pilot reached down and switched on the new-fangled radar, just to have a look. (Some pilots were reluctant to leave the radar on for long periods, for fear of being sterilized by unseen radiation. Remember, this was the early days of radar.)

Just as Captain C was about to conclude his oratory, the radar screen flashed alive and showed, unmistakably, a solid line of fierce, impenetrable storms . . . not somewhere far ahead, but barely three miles beyond the nose of the airplane.

Without thinking to release the little button on the public address mike, C shrieked at the co-pilot, "GET THIS SON OF A BLEEP OUT OF HERE, BEFORE WE HIT THAT BLEEP." This, of course, got the undivided attention of everyone in the airplane, as did the gut-wrenching, steep turn they felt as the co-pilot hastened to do his commander's bidding.

The flight then set a westerly heading in an attempt to fly around the west end of the weather. History does not record whether there even *was* a west end to the weather that night, but they did not find it, if it existed.

With fuel running perilously low, Captain C finally spotted a lighted runway and proceeded to land on it. A young flight line attendant, who had only seen pictures of a four engined airplane, watched in awe as the behemoth squealed to a halt and shut down. As the engines clattered and fell silent, Captain C slid open his window and shouted down, "What town is this?"

The passengers had had enough and began leaving the machine through whatever exit they could find and, without further invitation, headed for the nearest bar.

It wasn't until the next day that the local Greyhound bus agent in Waterloo, Iowa, found out how he came to send out a couple of full bus loads of passengers, mostly badly hung over, to Chicago.

Just a word here about Capt. C. You will meet him often in these pages, but despair not that he is out there on the line, waiting to thrill you. No one human could get in as much trouble as this guy, so I have lumped all of these adventures under the one title, Capt. C which stands for Captain Composite.

A SMOOTH FLIGHT

Tonight, though, our flight is smooth. The color of the sunset fades, and the electrical fireworks of the storm are left behind. Well below, the jewel-like nests of light that are the towns and villages of eastern Tennessee slip by. From your seat, you can easily recognize the planet Venus, dominating the vast starfield. Millions of light-years away, lying close to the western horizon, Venus is the brightest object to be seen. It is often mistaken for another airplane by even experienced pilots.

In your shirtsleeves, you are comfortable as you browse through a magazine and sip your drink. Just inches from your shoulder, the airstream is blasting past at 435 knots and the temperature is minus 59 degrees. Don't even try to figure the wind chill factor of those two figures...you would not want to be outside.

Glancing down, you notice that the towns are no longer visible, and the light from them is diffused by low cloud cover. Now you see milky pools of light glowing in the velvet blackness below.

A flight attendant stops by and offers you another drink, but you wisely decline. There is still some driving to be done, in Atlanta, and the police are getting justifiably cranky about drunk drivers. You are a long way from drunk and intend to stay that way, so you ask for coffee instead. The truth is that coffee won't alter the amount of alcohol in your system, but at least you won't be sleepy at the wheel.

THE CAUSES OF EAR PAIN

About the time you get your coffee, you feel a sharp pain in your ears. The airplane and the cabin pressure have started to descend.

Since this ear discomfort is common to every flight, and affects everyone to at least some degree, let's spend a little time on the subject.

The first word of advice is to stay on the ground and avoid flying if you are suffering from a cold, the flu or any form of congestion that would require the use of some decongestant or antihistamine. To fly when you have these symptoms goes far beyond mere discomfort. It can be downright dangerous and result in ruptured eardrums.

Your inner ear has canals and passages that admit air. Under normal circumstances—riding in an elevator, or driving up and down hills for example—the difference in air pressure between air outside your ear and that trapped inside the ear changes very gradually. The change may be noticeable, but is rarely painful. However, when you are aboard an airplane, changes in pressure occur more rapidly. Normally about 300 feet per minute is the rate of change.

As the airplane climbs to, say, 35,000 feet, the cabin pressure is reduced to an approximate 6000 feet. (RULE: As altitude increases, pressure decreases.) As the pressure outside of your ear decreases, the air pockets, let's call them "bubbles," begin to expand inside the ear. You may feel a slight "POP," but at this stage of the game, no real discomfort.

The problems begin during descent. As the airplane starts to lose altitude, the cabin is re-pressurized so that, upon landing, the air pressure outside the airplane and that inside are the same. As the airplane and the cabin pressure descend, the pressure must be increased.

The pockets inside your ear that were so happy to release their trapped air during climb are often reluctant to allow higher pressure air back into the ear. This is especially true if the inner ear passages are swollen or stopped up. Again, if you are congested, don't fly. If the pressure inside your ear cannot equalize with the pressure outside (cabin pressure), you may feel pain. However, there are tricks which can help.

The idea, in relieving ear pain, is to force the ear passages open, allowing pressure to equalize.

YAWN: Have you ever noticed, when yawning, that your ears seem to "turn on?" You have equalized air pressure inside and outside your ears. It works the same way in an airplane.

SWALLOW: This does about the same as yawning. Try it.

CHEW GUM: As in the above two examples, you are

flexing jaw muscles near your ears. This, in turn, flexes the passages leading to the inner ear, usually enough to equalize pressures. Keep doing these three things throughout the descent, and chances are that your ears will clear quite nicely. (If you are traveling with your boss, it may not be wise to yawn in his face without some word of explanation.)

THE VAL SALVA MANEUVER: This imposing sounding treatment should be used only as a last resort, and very, very carefully.

Close your mouth tightly, hold your nose, and begin to blow, gradually increasing pressure inside your head until you feel your ears clear. Try it right now. You can feel it even on the ground, without the danger of rupturing anything. If you, for any reason, have any discomfort doing this on the ground, or have any sort of persistent congestion, see your doctor before you get on an airplane.

GETTING READY TO LAND

"Folks, this is the captain. We are nearing the Atlanta airport and will be landing soon, so I will turn on the seatbelt sign now. Please fasten your seatbelt and observe the no-smoking sign when it appears just before landing. (I always feel a little silly saying that bit about the no-smoking sign. No matter how hard you "observe" the stupid sign, it will do nothing more than shine back at you. No further information or entertainment is to be had by "observation.")

"We hope you enjoyed your flight, and invite you to call us when you next plan air travel. The weather in Atlanta is overcast and foggy with a temperature of 62 degrees. Enjoy your stay."

What he did not tell you, is that the overcast layer of clouds is within 200 feet of the runway (pretty low), and the fog is restricting visibility to about ½ mile. You will fly an instrument approach, and he will "handfly" the airplane. Landings can be made in less than ¼ mile visibility; however, the approach must be flown by the auto-pilot even though all training and proficiency requirements have the pilot handflying down to 100 feet and ¼ mile. Any pilot worth his pay can nail 100 and ¼ all day long, with an engine out. Most pilots would prefer to handfly an approach just to keep in practice.

In the cabin, you notice the glare of the green navigation light in the fog outside of your window, and begin to feel the airplane maneuvering about. Soon you hear the flap motor begin to whine. You feel a momentary "floating" sensation. The wings, having been streamlined for high speed flight, are now being reshaped for the lower speeds required for the approach and landing by again lowering the flaps.

"NO-SMOKING." As you dutifully observe the sign, you feel the airplane's movements are a bit sharper — more noticeable. Up until now, your pilot has spent a great deal of effort keeping things as smooth as possible. Now, he must get serious about lining up his aircraft exactly with the runway. The earlier he does this in the approach, the smaller his corrections will be as he gets closer to the runway.

The rush of air and a bit of vibration, followed by a few, distinct thumps, now signal that landing gear has been lowered and locked in place. The flap motor hums again — more flaps. You feel a slight buffeting in the airplane. If you listen carefully, you may hear the engines change pitch slightly from time to time as the speed is adjusted to the exact value that the weight of the airplane requires. Your pilot has now prepared the machine for landing and has nothing to do but get it to the runway. Simple enough, right?

UP IN THE COCKPIT

Up in the cockpit, things seem quite relaxed, with no checklists being read and very little conversation. Quiet? Yes. Relaxed? Not really. All three crewmembers are concentrating on their individual tasks. Thier job is to fly an airplane, traveling over the ground at better than 150 MPH, through shifting wind currents, maintaining an exact course to the runway and an exact descent rate so as to be positioned to land when they actually see the runway. Any misalignment must be corrected within about six seconds.

Let's examine what takes place on a precision approach, and maybe it won't seem quite so impossible.

Two radio signals are being sent from the ground. One, called the "localizer," provides left/right guidance. The other, the "glideslope," gives up/down information. The signals from these two radios are received in the airplane and fed, through computer magic, to a large instrument directly in front of each pilot. This instrument, the flight director, combines several sources of information and is the main instrument used in the approach.

While the captain flies the machine, the first officer monitors his own flight director, constantly cross-checking the captain's instruments. These flight instruments are being fed by entirely separate sources, so that no one failure will affect both instruments. Any failure of any part of either instrument will result in a brightly colored "flag" that pops out and covers the affected part of the instrument. There is really not much chance that one of these flags could be missed. In addition to the flags, a bright yellow light comes on and warns both pilots that a "comparing computer" has sensed either a failure or a difference in the information each pilot is receiving. To back up all of this even further, the second officer, his work done on the rear panel, monitors both pilot's instruments and the progress of the approach. Before the approach was begun, he studied the approach chart. This poor fellow, on most airlines, is also a pilot who will be flying as soon as his seniority permits. However, on this flight, he must watch and has no controls with which to correct any mistakes he may observe. He is very quick to point out any discrepancies he sees, gloating all the while that, of course, he would never fly so ragged an approach.

THE APPROACH AND LANDING

Looking out at the wing, you see that the green navigation light (the one on the left wing is red, just as on all ships) is actually waving back and forth. Suddenly it stops. The pulsating glow is distracting to the pilots, and they have turned it from "flash" to "steady" to cease the annoyance.

You also notice wisps of vapor dancing along the top of the wing then trailing back in a twisting pattern. The moisture-laden air is racing over the top of the wing's surface, condensing out. Your wing is actually forming its own little clouds.

It has been almost three minutes since you heard the landing gear go down. Although you have been looking hard out of the window (good, you're helping) you have seen nothing. Suddenly you spot automobile lights on a highway, flashing past through a break in the fog, then some lights in a parking lot. Up front, they have seen nothing. While you have been looking straight down, the first officer has given one last look at his instruments, satisfied himself that the approach is "in the groove" and has "gone outside." He has transferred his eyes to the windshield in search of the real world—that loveliest of all sights, the runway lights. You have actually seen the parking lot long before he sees what he needs, because as you look only 200 feet, straight down, the first officer must look forward through about 3000 feet of mist, swirling past his windshield. He sees nothing but a brightening glow.

"ONE HUNDRED ABOVE," calls the captain, his attention fully on his instruments. He has announced that he is one hundred feet above his minimum descent altitude and if his trusty first officer, with his youthful, eagle-like eyes, does not soon announce the presence of the runway ahead, he will have to pull up and "go around."

"LIGHTS...RUNWAY DEAD AHEAD" The captain begins to look outside and the runway lights race to meet him. At first sight, the drizzle streaming back across the windshield tends to distort the light patterns he sees, but soon he can begin to use the lights of the runway to make any final corrections. He reaches up and turns on all of the landing lights. The glare of his own lights are intense, but he is now over the threshold of the runway. In the rushing confusion of mist racing past the windshield and the runway lights blurring by, he eases off the engines and lets the airplane settle onto the concrete. A slight bump...another, and you are down.

Things begin to happen rather quickly now. The panels on top of the wing, the spoilers, jump up and you feel the airplane settle a bit further. At the same time, you hear the engines being accelerated in reverse thrust...a harsher sound, but you can feel the machine slowing. Now a bit of wheel brakes—easy, the runway is damp and a little slippery. The full weight of the airplane is on the wheels, and you feel more brakes. When the spoilers are raised on the wing they effectively destroyed all the lift and allowed the airplane to settle fully on the wheels. If a pilot were to apply the brakes a little too firmly on a slick runway, the brake system has anti-skid protection. This produces a very jerky braking action, as the brakes are being released and rapidly reapplied.

On rare occasions, you may be startled to hear one or

more engines popping loudly. . .sort of a loud coughing noise. If you are seated next to the engines, the noise is quite loud and you may even see flashes of fire emitting from the front of the engine. This is unnerving, but really nothing to worry about. The name for this is "compressor stall," most commonly heard during reverse thrust operation on the landing roll out. On even rarer occasions, you may hear this sound during takeoffs in very strong crosswinds. The two side mounted engines on the 727 (called the "pod engines") gulp massive quantities of air straight into their intakes; however, the center, tail-mounted engine has to get its air through a twisting "S" duct. This air must strike the entry of this duct in a fairly straight direction, or the engine cannot get enough of the stuff of combustion, and literally "hiccups." Noisy, but harmless.

ON THE RUNWAY

As you turn off of the runway, the bright landing lights are turned off, and the flap motor starts its song again. The lights in the cabin brighten and you recall that, before landing, the cabin lights were very dim. The reason for this was to adapt the passengers' eyes to darkness. If, for any reason, there were a need to evacuate the airplane, all lighting in the cabin would have been lost with the exception of the self-powered emergency exit lights. With your eyes "night adapted," you could see and reach the exits more easily.

As the airplane approaches the gate, the flight attendant is chattering about something, but you feel pretty good — actually, you are delighted. You have survived an airplane ride, and nothing else can happen, right? Wrong!

An airplane has really great brakes and, on occasion, they must be used to avoid the various hazards of airport life — the suicidal drivers of all those little trucks and carts we mentioned. If you happen to be standing in the aisle when the captain is forced to brake hard, there is no maybe about it. You will fall. . .hard. The flight attendant has told you to remain seated until the airplane has come to a complete stop at the terminal. Believe her, and do it.

The chime sounds, the seatbelt sign goes off, and now you get up. It's over and if you have felt a little better about your flight as a result of this book, then we are both already

✈

ahead of the game. The odds are that you can fly regularly, for the rest of your life, and nothing worse than an overdone steak will ever trouble you.

THE GO-AROUND

Let's stop for just a moment and pretend we are watching all of this on a videotape. We are going to press the rapid rewind button. ZIP. You are back in your seat, buckling your seat belt and backing up. Out onto the runway, faster and faster, then the tail comes up slightly and you are swallowed again by the mist. STOP...Now press forward play again.

Looking down, you again see the lights on the highway, then the parking lot. You know that you are about to land when, suddenly, the engines wind up to full power, the nose of the airplane pitches up sharply and you again hear the sounds of the landing gear being retracted. You are not going to land after all and you are not pleased. What happened? Why are we going up again?

In the first place, there is no emergency aspect to this maneuver, called a "go-around." Even down to the last seconds before touchdown, a pilot must be prepared to abandon the landing and pull up for any number of reasons. Perhaps a chance gust of wind caught him just before he sighted the runway lights. When he did spot them, he did not like what he saw—a slight misalignment, a position that's a little low on the glideslope, or lights that simply don't look like he wants them to look. 200 feet up, and 150 MPH is no time to sit around scratchin' and thinkin'. The prudent pilot mutters something like, "Let's get out of here," and proceeds to get out of there. In reality, a "go-around" is much safer than a normal takeoff...you already have flying speed and even about 200 feet of altitude. It is the unexpected abruptness of the pull-up that startles people. When facing a tight approach, I try to alert my passengers to the possibility of a go-around so that they won't be taken by surprise.

A good captain, after he makes a go-around, will explain the situation, and reassure you that all is well with the airplane; but he will be a little busy for a few minutes, so don't expect an instant message from the cockpit.

THE PUBLIC ADDRESS SYSTEM

A word here about cabin announcements from the cockpit. Captains regard the use of the public address system in many different ways. Very few actually enjoy its use, for a very good reason...it's a hard thing to do. Pilots, as a rule, are not comfortable with the idea of public speaking. The task is made more difficult because, during an announcement, the speaker is talking to himself. No eye contact, and no idea as to how the words are being heard by the unseen audience. Things are always taking place in the cockpit that tend to distract a pilot, usually in mid-sentence. He must fight the urge to immediately direct his attention to the distraction.

"...We will be landing soon, the temperature in Miami ...what did he say, did he want us to level off at 7000 and ...(What was I saying to the people?)...Please call us when...there is another airplane over at two o'clock, is that the one he..." I try to make all of my cabin announcements when there is nothing else going on. I then fix my attention on a cloud formation outside the airplane and try to ignore what's going on inside.

There has been criticism leveled by some passengers who felt that some sort of emergency existed, and they did not receive immediate reassurance or instructions from the captain. Let's get something straight. If an emergency does exist, the pilot's first priority is to solve the problem...this is also his second, third and forth priorities. Besides, if a problem does exist, he is going to be a little excited himself, and that is going to show up in his voice if he does try to talk to you. That will not soothe...not even a little bit.

Perhaps actors Peter Graves and Robert Stack can deliver a calming little speech, while in the midst of cockpit chaos and confusion, but don't expect it from a real pilot in a real cockpit, at least not until things have settled down.

Along these same lines, TV commentators, when describing an air accident, end their reports with the phrase, "There was no report of trouble from the pilot of the doomed aircraft." The implication is that "the poor, dumb pilots never even knew that they were in trouble, or they would have provided some last words for your eager ears."

Nonsense. Of course the pilot knew what his troubles were and was busily engaged in trying to save his airplane and all aboard. The very last thought that would ever come into his mind would be to pick up a microphone and calmly reveal his problem, his corrective actions and their results. He would also know if his corrections were working. And he would have little inclination for providing the evening news with a posthumous quote, if the corrections weren't working.

The experts would know soon enough what happened, and the evening news people can wait for their findings.

A few captains regard an airplane full of hapless passengers as an audience for their own personal comedy routines, and a very few are really quite good at this. An equal few would rather grab a Texas rattlesnake by the neck than ever pick up that accursed microphone.

Give the man a break. Let him do his job of keeping you safe, then he will tell you what he can about what happened.

If the problem happened to be that a preceding airplane, on the approach, could not clear off of the runway before your man got there, you can expect that he will get downright testy with the control tower on his next approach. He will inform them that he does not need all that much practice in groping around through the Georgia fog, and when next he spots the runway, he expects to occupy it, all by himself.

Now we can "fast forward" you through another approach and, this time, a normal landing.

Your pilot cannot afford the luxury of believing that "it can never happen to him." While it usually doesn't happen to him, he must live in a "what if" world. What if this, that or the other were to happen? He must have procedures to cover anything that can happen, and a way to overcome any adversity. He has years of training and, more importantly, many more years of experience to call on.

But how about you? How prepared will you be if things start going a little abnormal? In the next chapter, we are going to be preparing you to ask yourself, "What if?"

CHAPTER 2

"WHAT IF...!"

In all honesty, this is not an easy subject to write about. There are so few emergencies, or even "alternate incidents," that there is not a real wealth of experience from which to draw. Things go along pretty smoothly for millions upon millions of flying miles, but sometimes things go wrong somewhere.

In a book that is supposed to convince you how safe it is to fly, it may seem strange that, in only the second chapter, we should concern ourselves with the things that can go wrong. However, to not do so would be to pretend that incidents never occur, that a million people, each day, never have anything worse than underdone chicken to complain about. If the odds were fair and absolute, you would have to fly regularly for a couple of lifetimes before anything of an emergency nature would ever catch up with you.

Sure, there will be mention made of some tragedies. You cannot very well have a book about aviation safety without this sort of thing. But we will not dwell on the accidents no one walked away from. We will concentrate on the things that you can do to insure that you will walk away.

When an incident, or accident, does occur, it rarely follows any book scenario. However if we amplify on the flight attendants' pre-flight briefing and the little safety information card located near every seat, perhaps you will be better prepared.

WHAT IF THERE IS AN EMERGENCY?

Airline crews are carefully trained to deal with emergencies and they will do their best to help all passengers in the event of an accident; however, there are are many factors which might prevent the crew from helping you. One or more of

✈

the crew may, themselves, be incapacitated. At best, there is only one cabin attendant assigned for every 49 passenger seats.

There may be some passengers who, for physical reasons, cannot help themselves. These people pose a special problem because the crew must inform them that they will be the last ones to be evacuated. This may not sound very fair-minded but during an emergency, being fair-minded means getting as many people out of the airplane as quickly as possible. It would not be fair to the other passengers for two flight attendants to block a narrow aisle in their attempt to carry an invalid to an exit, while many others waited patiently and possibly succumbed to smoke. Before the door closes on an airliner, the captain is given an accurate account of the number of passengers on board. If he were to be forced to evacuate the ship, he would want to see that same number of people outside of the airplane after the excitement died down.

No, gentle reader, the one person on the scene of an accident most able to help you is you. By controlling panic (usually unjustified panic) and planning your actions ahead of time, you stand a much better chance of walking away from almost any situation.

Let's forget the word "accident," and concentrate on "incident" instead. There are, again, two kinds of incidents: planned and unplanned. This does not imply that each airline has a department devoted to planning incidents. The planned incident simply gives everyone time to think things out.

IS THE INCIDENT PLANNED OR UNPLANNED?

In a planned incident, the captain advises you that a problem exists, that he and his crew are trying to work it out and, in the meantime, he asks the cabin crew to begin preparations for an emergency landing.

As an example, let's use the emergency most beloved of third rate television script writers. The old "landing gear won't come down" scene. (This gives them time to develop in-depth character studies of some of the passengers — in peril, and some of the crew — during stress). As you will see in the technical chapter discussing the hydraulic system, this example is pretty much academic, since the landing gear is designed to extend without any help at all. But

Hollywood loves it and you do go to the movies, don't you?

Applying the same example to the unplanned emergency, the landing gear would simply collapse after landing, with no warning. In this case, everyone is going to have to be very creative in dealing with the problem as it develops. No time for warnings or briefings is available, and the passenger who has thought about how he would get out, even though things are going smoothly, would be light-years ahead of the one who is still buried in *The Wall Street Journal*.

In the first, planned incident, the pilot would keep the airplane aloft as long as possible to try and find a procedure that will successfully lower the recalcitrant landing gear. The cabin attendants have ample time to re-brief the passengers and prepare them for a gear-up landing. Newspeople love to call such a landing, a crash landing. Nonsense! When a pilot knows that he must belly land an airplane, you can bet that it will be the most controlled landing of his career. It should also comfort you to know that no one has ever been hurt in such a gear-up landing. Keep that fact in mind.

In the unplanned incident, everyone is surprised at the same time. There is no time for briefings or even for you to take out the little safety card and locate the nearest emergency exit. You will have all you can do to clear your mind of the paralysis of panic and begin to act. If you start acting without some plan in mind, you can just as easily be doing the wrong thing.

LISTEN TO THE FLIGHT ATTENDANTS' BRIEFING

O.K. Let us just stay with the balky landing gear, and get down to business. LISTEN TO THE FLIGHT ATTENDANTS' BRIEFING. Maybe you have heard it all before. Heard it, yes, but how long has it been since you listened to it, and thought about it? Take out that little safety information card and read it. Look around the cabin and find the emergency exit nearest to your seat. Look at it and determine what type of exit it is: an overwing window or a regular door? Look back at the little card and study how you would open that exit. (Each exit has its own method of opening and can differ on different types of airplanes.) Having done that, now find another, secondary exit on the opposite side of the airplane. You cannot depend on being able to use your primary selection; it could be jammed, or there could be fire outside. Perhaps everyone else has the same idea of using your primary exit. Go immediately to your secondary exit. THINK...AND KEEP ON THINKING.

HOW TO OPEN THE "PLUG" DOOR

Here is something that none of these briefings or safety information cards even mention, and I've always thought was very important. All doors and exits on modern jet airliners open inward, before they can be pushed outward and completely opened. Confusing? Listen. When the jets came along, they started flying at very high altitudes, requiring higher cabin pressures. No matter how strong, or how many locking lugs were put on doors that opened outward, every once in a while a door would pop open and all the pressurization would rush out, along with anything, or anyone, near it. Not good.

So the designers went to work and created the "plug" door. On the long, vertical sides of the door, the door is larger than the door frame, while the top and bottom are slightly smaller than the frame. The door is outside the airplane while opened, then it is slipped sideways through the smaller frame when being closed. Once the entire door is inside of the airplane, it is rotated, by some clever hinge geometry, until it goes back out against the doorframe. *Voilà!* The door is now held closed by the pressure inside the airplane.

The catch to all of this engineering wizardry is that to open the door, it must move inward slightly before it can be pushed back through the frame and opened. The problem is to move the door inward if a lot of panicky people are trying their best to push outward on the door. DO NOT CROWD AGAINST THIS DOOR. Let someone get the door open fully.

THE EVACUATION SLIDE

On each main door of an airplane, there is an evacuation slide, neatly packaged in a fiberglass housing. As soon as the airplane is ready to leave the gate, a flight attendant will take a metal bar from the housing and attach it to some fittings in the cabin floor. The evacuation slide is attached to this bar. Now, if the door is opened, the housing will fall away, the slide will fall out the doorway and begin inflating with compressed air. If the slide were not to begin to inflate automatically, it could be inflated by pulling a handle on the slide package. These handles are clearly marked and distinctively colored in some high-visibility red or orange.

If you need to pull this handle, make sure that the slide package is outside the airplane's doorframe, because the slide is pretty dumb. It does not know if it is in or out, but is going to inflate anyway. A slide inflated inside an airplane takes up a lot of room. It will then be impossible to push the slide out the doorway. The slide is as strong as it is dumb. It can easily hurt people and very effectively block its doorway. This door cannot be used as an exit once the slide blocks it.

Capt. C was sitting placidly in his cockpit one bright morning, expounding on some subject of which he had little knowledge, awaiting the command to start engines when a flight attendant burst in, grabbed the fire axe, and ran shrieking back down the aisle. Ol' C twisted around just in time to watch the flight attendant attacking what appeared to be a writhing, yellow dragon. At the same time, a passenger was howling something about, "She's killin' Egbert... My Gawd, she's killin' my kid." Mortally wounded, the dragon began to sag pitifully, and the flight attendant dropped her weapon, dove under the hissing folds of yellow fabric and dragged a thoroughly terrified Egbert out and presented him to the hysterical mother. It seems that the fiberglass housing had fallen aside just enough for the handle to become visible. That was all that Egbert needed. He had broken away from Mommy, and pulled it, while it was inside of a closed door.

Capt. C arose and slowly approached the woman, his eyes burning with the very real suggestion of homicide, and he reached down to pick up the axe. (He later swears that he was merely going to return it to the cockpit, where it belonged.) The woman renewed her screams, grabbed her little darling and left the airplane quickly, presumably to become a loyal customer of Amtrak.

THE OVER-WING EMERGENCY EXITS

If opening the regular doors is a problem, the over-wing emergency exits can be even worse. These large doors are ✈

not hinged at all but, when unlatched, simply fall inward. There is a proper way to open and stow these exits, and it is described on the card. Normally, a crewmember will open these exits if he can get to them. In an unplanned incident, usually the crew cannot reach these exits because of the crowd, so you must be prepared to open the exit yourself. Read the card and memorize the procedure. Do this on each flight.

During a planned emergency, you have more time to orient your exits and plan. The flight attendants will seat what they call an able-bodied person next to the window exit and very carefully explain its operation. At no time will an invalid be seated near an emergency exit. That is federal law and is common to all airlines.

PREPARING FOR AN EMERGENCY TOUCHDOWN

The flight attendants will tell you to take all sharp objects out of your pockets. Put them in a coat pocket. You will again be briefed on the proper position to assume just before touchdown: leaning forward and putting your head on your crossed arms which rest on the seat in front of you. You might also extend your legs as far as possible. The idea here is to prevent any of your parts from being thrown forward during deceleration. Let your seatbelt take the strain, it's designed for it. Stay seated until the airplane comes to a complete stop, then unfasten your seat belt.

It may sound silly to dwell on a subject as simple as unfastening your seatbelt, but the truth of the matter is that in virtually every evacuation incident, someone forgets to unfasten the seatbelt, tries to get up, and can't. Then he freezes, unable to do anything further. He simply forgot. Practice this simple act a few times every time you board an airliner, then think about what you did. About half the people who have to be rescued by the crew are sitting there, in their seats, with belts fastened and bewildered looks on their faces. They have reached a point where something did not happen as they wished it to (standing up) and their minds simply stopped functioning. Don't let this happen to you. Keep thinking ahead about each detail of your plan to get out of the airplane.

A good idea, if time permits, and if your landing will be in a winter environment, is to put on one warm coat before the landing. You do not want to be so bulky that getting through a window exit will be a problem, but it could be several minutes before anyone reaches you with any blankets or other sources of warmth. If you do not do this before the landing, do not try to put on a coat after the landing. Get out!

In fact, do not take anything whatsoever with you. No carry-on luggage, fishing rods or portable radios. NOTHING! Just get the hell out. If it isn't yelling and squirming and calling you Daddy or Mommy, don't try to take it off the airplane. You must keep your hands free to help you get out.

Along this line of thought, if you are taking special medication, keep a small supply of this medication *on your person*. Not in a purse or briefcase which you will not be allowed to take with you, but in a pocket. This is especially important if the need for your medicine could be triggered by a tramatic incident—like a belly landing.

The actual touchdown is going to be anti-climactic. You will be told by a crewmember when the approach has begun, and you take your position. Down to the runway, the captain will hold the airplane off the concrete as long as he can. The touchdown will be smooth. Most people who have ridden through a gear up landing describe the touchdown as very gentle. However, soon the deceleration begins to build and becomes very pronounced. You are scrubbing off a lot of energy with the belly of the machine. You will also notice the noise, which can get downright dramatic. If you are facing a window, you may see what seem to be explosions of flashing lights. The airplane is sliding over runway lights, destroying them. Early in the slide, it is possible that you may hear a loud explosion. If one wheel is partly exposed to the abrasive concrete, a tire might explode.

After what may seem like an eternity, but in reality is more like 10 seconds, there is a very definite stop. This airplane has served its usefulness and is not going any further. Let's leave.

GETTING OUT AFTER THE TOUCHDOWN

Every new airplane, before the FAA will let it fly, must demonstrate its ability to be evacuated completely, within 90 seconds, using only half of the exits installed. Each airline which buys this airplane must also demonstrate that its training is such that its cabin and cockpit crews are capable of doing the same. There is no warning as to which exits will be unusable. All windows are frosted and the "passengers" are served dinner. The passengers are usually clerks and agents or mechanics and their families. No flight personnel are allowed. Sometime during the meal, the lights go out, the cabin begins to fill with smoke (harmless) and someone starts shouting, "evacuate the airplane." At the same time, the FAA turns on flashing red lights, placed after the passengers boarded, to simulate fire outside half the exits. These exits cannot be used. The last person, including the crew, must be off of the airplane within 90 seconds, but it is a real scramble.

SMOKE IN THE CABIN

The point can also be made that, in the event of smoke during a real emergency, it will not be of the non-toxic variety. It will be real. The only thing to do, in the case of smoke, is to cover your mouth and nose with a handkerchief, some napkins or even a torn shirt, anything to filter the particles of smoke. You can also try to stay low, crouching, as you exit the airplane.

Smoke in the cabin is very rarely a problem, at least in situations such as this one. Studies have been underway for a long time to try and remove the sources of cabin smoke, which are usually the fiber glass wall paneling, the foam seat cushions or insulation within the walls. I will have more to say about this later. The real restriction to visibility may be dust.

Over the years, dust accumulates in hidden nooks and crannies, just as it does at home. A lot of this dust will be dislodged during the slide to a stop and can reduce visibility.

CARRY-ON DEBRIS

Even worse than dust is carry-on debris. Anything in the overhead bins could possibly come crashing down and form a real obstacle course. Any solid object, briefcase, hanger bag or the like, can give someone a real headache, either when it comes flying out of the overhead bin, or when it becomes a very unstable mess upon which to try to walk.

Time permitting, the crew should try to remove everything, even pillows and blankets, from the overhead compartments. A blanket is not going to hurt anyone as it bops them on the head, but lying on the floor it can easily trip someone. That person goes down, forming an even larger obstacle...another person falls...then another. Get the picture? Here, though, the catch phrase is "if time permits."

MOVE QUICKLY AND CALMLY

Get up and start moving with your plan toward the exit you have selected, but go with the flow of other passengers. If they are moving then there is an open exit that is allowing them to leave the airplane. Don't try to fight your way upstream. Keep thinking. Is a crowd gathering at that exit? Is the exit opening? If not, start looking at your secondary exit. How about it? Crowded? Open? When one is open, go for it. Move quickly but calmly.

Perhaps the most important piece of advice in this book is: DO NOT PUSH AND DO NOT LET YOURSELF BE PUSHED! If you start pushing someone, the very best you can hope for is that he or she will turn around and paste you one on the kisser. The worst is that he or she may go down, and you will trip over the body, then someone else is going to trip over you. Next thing you know, you are at the bottom of a twisting pile of people, in a narrow aisle, with other people climbing over you. This is not the tidy way to get out of an airplane. Do not push anyone in front of you, especially near an unopened door or exit. Remember, the door must come in before it can go out and open.

If someone starts pushing you, hang on to seatbacks, arm rests or anything except someone else. Anything to keep you on your feet. This is why you need both hands free. When you get to the exit, use it, or you will have footprints all over your back, and probably a crew member will simply boot you in the rear. He or she is not trying to make friends right now, but trying to get you out.

USING THE SLIDE

If one of those slide things has been deployed, remember what you saw on the safety information card. Jump just far enough out to clear the door frame and land on the old buns. Slide down to the end and keep moving away from the slide. Don't stand there, because you are about to be hit by the next person down the slide. Keep moving away from the airplane, find a gathering group and join them. Stay with them for two reasons.

1. Someone is going to want to count noses to make sure no one is missing.

2. Very soon the runway is going to be alive with every emergency vehicle in fourteen counties. There is going to be more dust than you have ever seen, and flashing lights by the hundreds. Visibility will not be good, especially with all those trucks. Look at it this way: you have survived a genuine belly landing and you've got one whale of a story to tell for the next 20 years. The airline is going to offer you all kinds of goodies and you don't want to spoil it by getting run over by a fire chief in a little red truck. Groups are easier to spot by excited emergency people.

STAY CALM AFTER IT'S ALL OVER

Now, standing there, looking at that crippled bird, with all the rescue people scurrying about, the flashing lights, you can let your mind start racing. You've just joined a very elite and a very small group of people. Not more than a few hundred people have gone through what you just have, excluding those on TV dramas. It will do no good at all to start a lot of negative thinking. Forget what could have been — it wasn't. Likewise, it serves no purpose to start getting angry, at least until you know with whom you should be angry and, at this time, no one knows. There will be plenty of time for that later. Do not start demanding answers to questions that, for the moment, cannot be answered. The flight crew, especially, is going to be more than a little curious as to why the airplane did not operate as it should have.

There will be all sorts of investigations and blame will be assigned where it belongs. For now, thank whatever deity you choose, and maybe the crew. See if you can find some humor in the whole thing, then walk away. Remember, no one has ever been seriously hurt in one of these belly landings. Then go get on another airplane, the sooner the better. You have just had proof positive that the system works: the procedures work.

That pretty well takes care of the most dramatic incident in which you can ever be involved, but probably won't be involved in.

There is another item that the flight attendant talks about in her briefing that you should spend a little time thinking about. Again, you can fly for a theoretical half a billion miles before it becomes probable that something like this will happen to you, but, what if...!

DEPRESSURIZATION

DEPRESSURIZATION: You are comfortably sipping on your second cocktail, browsing over the latest sales figures of your company, and generally feeling pretty good about things. Suddenly, your ears begin to pop and the air around you begins to "mist." Something is happening to the pressurization, and the air in the cabin is beginning to "climb." You have heard that you can't breathe the thin air of high altitude for very long. You remember the flight attendant saying something about oxygen masks, but you don't remember what it was. The airplane begins to pitch down in a dive. You feel a shudder start to shake the whole machine.

THE OXYGEN MASK

Just about the time you are thoroughly confused and beginning to feel a bit of old-fashioned fright, POP, a little door, just above your seat, opens and two or three yellow "cups" and a lot of plastic tubing appear before your very eyes.

The very first thing you want to do is sit back in your seat and breathe normally. Don't gasp for air, and don't try to hold your breath because you can't do it, and you can cause your internals some real mischief if you try. Breathe normally. If you are smoking, put out your cigarette. One of the dumber things you can do, in this life, is to try to put an oxygen mask over your nose and mouth, while you have a cigarette between your lips. It is a very effective way to alter your looks, considering the explosive nature of oxygen.

When the little door opens, reach up, grasp the mask nearest you (if you are in an aisle seat, go for the mask nearest the aisle), and pull the mask down to your face. Don't try to stretch you neck and take your face up to the mask. A short piece of string is attached to the mask, and to a little valve that prevents oxygen from flowing until the mask is pulled away from the door. If that little string does not release the valve, no oxygen will flow to the mask. In some of the newer airplanes these masks may appear from the seat-back in front of you.

Pull the mask down to you face, cover your nose and mouth with it, and continue to breathe normally. You have already done all you can do to protect yourself, and, if you see the need, you can help your neighbor. If you are traveling with children, get your own mask on first, then help them. If you were to pass out, you would not be of much use to them, and they are not going to be able to help you.

THE PLANE WILL DESCEND TO LOWER ALTITUDES

The truth is that, even without oxygen, you would most likely not totally lose consciousness for more than a minute or so. Remember the diving sensation and the shudder in the aircraft? The pilot has already been alerted to the loss of cabin pressure. His procedure includes getting the airplane down to an altitude where the oxygen masks are not necessary for sustaining life. With the engines reduced to idle thrust, the speed brakes extended (those spoiler panels also act as speed brakes and cause the shudder), and the airplane pointed down, it will come down from high altitude like a free falling brick. Within about four minutes, the airplane can descend to 10,000 feet, the altitude at which you can breathe normally.

Again, as is the case in most fast-developing problems, don't expect a monologue from the pilot on what to do. You must do it yourself. The pilot's first priority is to continue flying the airplane and to try to solve the problem. This keeps the crew pretty busy. You don't want to distract them. They will explain the situation to you once they have ensured your safety. . . and not until.

To summarize:

1. Put out any smoking material.

2. Reach up and pull down the mask nearest you, cover your nose and mouth with the mask.

3. Breathe normally, not gasping or trying to hold your breath.

4. Help your children, or neighbor, if that is necessary.

5. Sit back and try to relax. You've done all you can.

PARTIAL DECOMPRESSION

This procedure was designed to cope with what is called "Explosive Decompression" such as the case when a large window or door blows out. In jet airliners designed in the last twenty-five years, this has not happened more than once or twice. Partial decompressions do occur on rare occasions, usually when one air conditioning system (these also pressurize the airplane) fails. The remaining air conditioning system may not maintain enough pressure to prevent the masks from falling automatically from the overhead panels, but the slightly reduced pressure is not a serious health risk. The pilot will descend quickly to an altitude where even one system can provide a comfortable level of pressurization. Therefore, even if those little yellow masks should make an unexpected appearance, the odds are very good that they aren't really needed. But don't assume this . . . use them anyway.

MOTION SICKNESS

MOTION SICKNESS: This is not really as much of a problem these days, as it used to be, what with high flying jets being able to fly over most weather. In the old days, when the low, slow propeller planes encountered bumpy air, they could be in it for extended periods of time. The vertical pitching motions can get to the traveler who is unaccustomed to them, and that includes most of us. The inner ear is the culprit here, at least in the case of those who really suffer from motion discomfort.

Most people who actually lose their lunch during a normal flight only do so because they have conditioned themselves to believe that this is what is going to happen. Once convinced that turning green is a personal prerequisite to every flight, then it becomes one, no matter how smooth the flight. These people are going to get sick—period. They feel entitled to it.

Many of these same people feel much better if they take Dramamine, or some other anti-motion sickness drug, before a flight. Again, they have been convinced that science has provided a quick cure for their problems in the shape of a little pill. If many of these people could be convinced that aspirin or a sip of Coke would help, it probably would, but only if they got this information from someone they trusted enough to cast aside their own preconceptions.

There are some who are quite responsive to drugs, and they should continue to take them. However, the simple truth is that there are darn few airplane rides these days that are as rough as a cab ride across the potholes of virtually any city in the world.

There is one trick that some seasoned travelers use that seems to work. Open the little vent above your seat fully, put a pillow behind your shoulders, then lean back so that your face is pointing straight up. Let me explain what you are doing. Normal movements, the ones that you live with each day, are usually fore and aft, and side to side. Your inner ear is accustomed to these planes of movement and deals with them constantly. However, with the exception of some high speed elevator rides, those vertigo producing ear canals rarely have to contend with vertical movements. They can be trained to do so. Sailors train their ear canals all of the time.

By leaning your head back, you are fooling the inner ear canals into thinking that the vertical motions that they are protesting are really fore and aft motions. They are much happier with this idea. At the same time you can fix your eyes on some spot inside the cabin. This reduces the "swimming" sensation.

Above all, if someone near you starts to to get "uncomfortable," don't watch, or you are finished for certain, and may as well get that little bag handy. You know the one I mean...it tells you how to get sick in four languages. Another trick that the writer's wife uses is to dab a bit of perfume on her upper lip if things start getting really bumpy and someone near her starts to turn green. This perfume trick also works if you find the smell of the airplane objectionable. Some people do.

SKYJACKING

SKYJACKING: This is a simple subject to address. If you happen to be aboard an airliner that gets...uh...sidetracked, simply do what you are told by whoever is in charge. The person with a weapon is always in charge. The thing you do not do is try to be a hero.

THE PURPOSE OF THIS BOOK

If we have accomplished anything with this chapter, it is to point out to you that there are no fast and simple rules or regulations for dealing with an emergency. You are the one most able to help yourself when something starts happening, and you can only do this if you are able to continue thinking rationally and logically in the face of confusing circumstances. This is not always the easiest thing in the world to do. Confusion—what's happening, why is it happening, what's being done to correct all of these things that are baffling to me? You must learn to accept the fact that, in an airplane particularly, things are going to happen that you won't understand. But just because you don't understand them, does not mean that there is no one aboard who does. What may seem frightening to you can be the most normal thing in the world for the crew, who see these things every day of their lives. That is the reason I am writing this book, to try to expose you to the normal, routine things that you do not experience in your everyday life, but that will happen on every flight, as well as exposing you to a few "what ifs." If you are going to be nervous on an airplane, try to save your nervousness until it is justified.

Once you have experienced frightening things a few times, they will no longer frighten you. You may not understand what's happening, but since it happened before and you survived, you begin to trust that maybe someone else did know what was happening and how to cope with it.

ENGINE TORCHING

If you are riding on one of the large, "wide body" airplanes, you may observe the un-nerving sight of smoke, even flame, pouring from the rear of one of the wing mounted engines. Explanation: In order to save fuel, it is common practice to leave the gate without all the engines running. The captain does not need them all to taxi, however, as he nears the take-off runway, he will start the remaining engines.

Some oil normally collects in the lower sections of the engine and when the heat of starting occurs, this oil will really start smoking. On rare occasions there will be a small amount of fuel there also and you will see flame. The starting process is proceeding normally and the flame will soon be blown away by the engines' exhaust, however, if you happen to be watching one of your engines blazing merrily away...! This is known as "torching" and is fairly common.

On a gusty evening in New York, this happened. Some passengers witnessed flame coming from one of the engines, decided that the plane was on fire and panicked. One started yelling and jumped for a door. He pulled the emergency door handle and the door opened, deploying the slide. Several passengers followed him and they all slid out into the night, from a moving airplane. They slid directly into the blast of the now running engine, but none were

➤

seriously injured.

In the cockpit, a door open warning light appeared and the captain ordered his second officer to check the door while he continued to start the engines for take-off. Soon, however, a flight attendant raced into the cockpit and announced that people were jumping out of the airplane.

The sight of flames on an airplane is unwelcome, but wait until someone tells you to leave. Had the fire been real and presented a danger to the passengers, sensors would have signalled the cockpit and the captain would have stopped the machine and ordered an evacuation.

Don't be too hasty in deciding to take matters into your own hands. It gets doggone lonesome, standing in the middle of a dark airport, watching your flight trundle off into the night without you.

Most folks are not very comfortable with having to have blind faith in someone else, especially in someone they do not know. People like to have control of their lives, at least when confronted with what they perceive to be a life-threatening situation. When one is faced with open-heart surgery, or some other critical operation, one can shop around for a surgeon who inspires confidence. It is not required that the patient know exactly how the operation is to be performed or what techniques or equipment are to be used, but he or she can gain some insight into the doctor's ability, simply by talking with him. It is a perceived confidence, to be sure. If one is not a surgeon, one is not likely to really know how efficient another surgeon will be, during a given operation. Your operation. If you cannot feel a level of confidence in a surgeon, you are free to find another who makes you feel better.

Another perceived life threatening situation, to many people, is flying. Let's face it, to the average air traveler, one who climbs on an airplane once or twice a year, the scenes of carnage he or she sees on television are the most exposure to air travel that they will receive during a lifetime. But you rarely have an opportunity to meet the captain before a flight and to get any sort of a feeling for his abilities. A person's image of an airline crew may very well be based on some TV drama or, even worse, the *Airplane* series of movies. You file on board with all the other people and are met with a closed cockpit door...a little closet that you know is full of technology and magic. There are at least two people up there who would presume to take you into a hostile environment. You wish you could get some feel for their competence, but you can't. For this reason, I insist that the cockpit door be left open during the passenger boarding process. At least my passengers can look in and see real, live human beings. Most crews will welcome anyone who wants to stop in and say hello, so do it. It may help your frame of mind to have a few words with the crew, ask about the weather, how high or fast you will be flying, anything to establish that they are relaxed and do not consider this flight a threat at all. If the crew is not apprehensive, why should you be? You are all in the same boat, aren't you?

At the opening of this chapter, I stated that this was not an easy subject on which to write. Abnormalities, like cabin depressurization and belly landings, occur so rarely that there are very few individuals who have experienced them. Flight crews practice and practice, then they go out on the line and everything works right. Flight after flight, year after year, all of those procedures that you have learned so well, lay collecting dust in some dark corner of the mind.

Occasionally, something like this does happen, but it always happens to some other guy on some other airline. You hear the rumors, perhaps see an article or even a picture in the paper. Months later, your own airline issues a bulletin that describes what happened and any changes in procedure that the incident has inspired.

Then, one night. . .

REALITY: RETRACTED LANDING GEAR

On the evening of January 17th, 1986, the writer was approaching Washington National airport from the northwest. The night air was calm and smooth and we delayed lowering the landing gear both to save fuel and to reduce the noise a bit to the Washington suburbs below.

The "River Approach," as it is called, is one of the most beautiful approaches to any airport. The airplane drifts down the Potomac River with the Georgetown area to the left and the Pentagon off to the right. Closer in is the National Cathedral, the Watergate and the Kennedy Center for the Performing Arts out the left, then the monuments of Lincoln and Washington.

"Gear down—final checklist," the first officer called.

➤

I reached over and lowered the large handle that drops the landing gear. There followed the reassuring rush of air and the slight jolt as the nose landing gear was released from its up-lock, just below the cockpit.

"No-smoking sign."

"On."

"Landing gear..." We waited. It usually takes a few seconds for the main gear to lock down. Four red lights were glowing showing that the right, left and nose wheels were in transit. Another jolt. Green lights appeared indicating that the left main and nose gear had locked in place. Then the "doors" light went out. The gear doors had closed.

"Captain, we have an unsafe right main," the second officer announced. He did not really have to say it. We were all looking at the bright red glow.

"Keep the approach going," I told the first officer. "I'll re-cycle it."

The gear retracted smoothly and I lowered the handle again.

"Damn."

We pulled up away from the traffic pattern and for the next thirty minutes we executed, then repeated, every procedure in the book to get rid of that bloody red light. Nothing worked. I had one trick I still could try. Touch down on the runway and try to shake the stubborn wheel down. It was a lousy trick and I did not know if anyone had successfully done it. An unknown.

Finally, with fuel, time and ideas running out all at the same time, I was forced to make the most difficult decision of more than thirty years of flying. I had to land my aircraft with the gear retracted. I had to deliberately damage an airplane, however there was less danger to the passengers this way and that had to be the only priority. We headed the airplane toward Dulles International Airport which has the longest, smoothest runways in the area.

"Gear up. We are going to belly the beast."

The landing went smoothly and the procedures worked well. 137 passengers and a crew of eight were evacuated in just under one minute. There were no injuries.

Later, I would reflect that the landing had gone exactly like the one described in the beginning of this chapter, written almost a year before. There were things that I would have done differently. I sincerely wish that time had permitted me to give a more detailed briefing to my passengers on what to expect. Perhaps this could have soothed some anxieties, but my first priority had to be concentrating on the landing itself.

I also had to ponder, after poking a little good natured fun at the odds makers, statisticians and television script writers, that perhaps fate is the hunter, as Gann has suggested so eloquently. Less than a dozen pilots have ever had to make the decision that faced me that Friday evening. I had written about the experience, then had to do it. Had I attracted that great genie of fate by writing these words?

There were a few minor deviations from the landing as described in this chapter. The touchdown was smooth but the noise was not as dramatic as I had expected. Perhaps it was more pronounced in the cabin as our 140,000-pound airplane scrubbed away 130 miles per hour. The stop was also gentler than I had anticipated. I had recalled a film of another belly-landing that showed the runway lights exploding beneath the sliding airplane, creating a fire hazard, so I deliberately landed slightly to one side of the center of the runway. There were no exploding lights.

The escape slides all inflated properly. With the airplane lying on its belly, however, the angle of the slides was rather shallow. This made it difficult for the passengers to reach the bottom. Many passengers, unable to scoot their way to the end, merely rolled off the side of the slides. Whatever works. In the cabin, I was unable to observe this. After everyone had left the aircraft and I had made a quick inspection to see that no one was left aboard, I appeared at the main entry door and followed the proper procedure. My exit was a little less than dignified. I hopped out and hit the slide dead center. Dead center was where I stayed, sprawled in the middle of that great yellow tube, going nowhere. It was then that I discovered the technique of rolling off the side.

There was virtually no dust. Nothing fell from the overhead cabinets. There was a small layer of smoke that entered the cabin from outside. There was no fire, but the friction of our grinding stop had created some slight smoke. Any wind at all would have dissipated this smoke before it entered the cabin; however, we had no wind.

Very few passengers used the over-wing exits even though these were open. People were moving so quickly

➤

and smoothly to the door exits that few saw the need to crawl out of a little hole. Still, we were able to evacuate 137 passengers in just under one minute.

About the worst aspect of the whole business was the fact that the passengers were besieged by members of the media when they arrived at the terminal. It took about two hours for the NTSB to release the personal belongings of the passengers from the cabin and, since the airplane was resting on its belly for about ten hours, their checked luggage did not reach them (delivered by cab to their homes) until the next morning.

That made me feel pretty good. The worst that had happened to my passengers was having to face a lot of TV cameras and some disrupted dinner plans. My crew had worked well together. We simply did a job that had to be done, then we put it behind us. That also made me feel pretty good.

The dusty procedures were no longer an abstract. They were real and they had worked.

O.K., let's meet this crew, or at least let's meet a composite of what you will see is a group that possesses legendary independence.

CHAPTER 3

THE PEOPLE

It is no more possible to categorize airline pilots than any other group of people. Pilots, like every other collection of humans, come in all shapes, sizes, colors and sexes. Some play tennis while others race cars. Some regard sailing as the only civilized way to spend off-duty hours while others awaken with the first winter snow and consider time not spent sliding down a hill on a pair of expensive boards as wasted. They drive Cadillacs and VWs. One captain I once knew boasted that he had never spent more than $200 for any car, but would buy two or three junkers at a time. He did this on the theory that when he walked out of the house to go to work, at least one of his heaps would start. When one failed to do so that was the end if it, and he moved on to the next one. Sort of a perverse kind of redundancy.

There is a thread of commonality which all pilots share: their love for what they are doing. Flying. They are well-paid, but money is not the reason they are in the cockpit. Money allows them to live comfortably between flights, but flying, itself, is life.

This love of flight is not easy for a non-flier to understand. To most folks, work is what you must do to live whatever lifestyle you have chosen to live. A person, seeking success, may join a country club so that he can play golf with the "right" people and increase his own success. A pilot may belong to that same country club, but he joined to play golf. Period. You will rarely find him at the social events, or draped over the bar scheming to meet Mr. Big. In short, the pilot is perfectly content with what life has dealt him. His only interest in Mr. Big is what kind of golfer he is.

The importance of this is that you, the passenger, know that the man in command of your flight is there because he really wants to be there. It is a simple fact that anyone who truly loves his work is going to do a better job of it. However, the road to that captain's seat is not a short one, nor is it an easy one.

THE PILOT'S TRAINING

There are a few captains, mostly flying large airplanes for the major airlines, who began their careers during WW II; but the majority of the pilots that you will encounter started flying during the '50s or early '60s. Their training was largely military, which is the best initial training a pilot can have, and their early experience was with the service. Others earned their wings as "ag pilots" (crop dusters) or as charter pilots at a thousand little strips across the land. All were good, in their own way, long before they were accepted by the airlines. No one has a better feel for an airplane than that crop duster, who learned his trade in the early morning hours, flying just a few scant feet above the high lines and fences of southern Louisiana. No pilot has learned instrument flying techniques better than the commuter pilot, winding his way through the fog shrouded mountains of Pennsylvania. As for real precision, look to the Navy pilot who, low on fuel, must plant a jet fighter on the pitching, rolling deck of an aircraft carrier out in the North Atlantic. He must do it right, the first time and every time. He won't get a lot of second tries at a carrier.

No, there are no beginners among those who walk into the personnel offices of America's airlines, but those few who make it through all the testing and interviews, the physicals and screening, must start all over again.

Initial training begins with a week or two in classes designed to teach the fledgling aviator the airline's own rules and regulations. He is given a small library of manuals that will become his Bibles for the rest of his career. Forms and other bits of corporate and government information are introduced to him. Someone's motel room becomes the semi-official after-hours study hall, and midnight oil burns freely.

Then comes the airplane, or at least some mention of an airplane. The "new hire," as he is called, will be assigned a partner and an instructor. Each day, the students will sit down, for an hour or so, at a slide/tape machine that will expose them to the airplane they will fly as flight engineers. They will study the machinery one system at a time. Every switch, warning light and instrument will be explained. After the slide/tape machine, the students go into the "cardboard cockpit." This trainer is an accurate representation of the airplane's cockpit, with switches, lights and a few simulated instruments that work. The schedule is an hour at the slides and two hours in the cardboard box. (Time moves more quickly with switches and lights to play with.)

After about six weeks of learning procedures, procedures and more procedures, the trainee is ready for the real simulator. Known simply as "the box," the simulator is, in every respect, a real airplane. The box, mounted on spider-like legs, pitches, rolls and shakes just like the real thing. Every instrument and switch tells the same story and the trainee gets the same reaction that he would get in the airplane. He feels the tar strips in the taxiway, as the nose gear and then the main gear pass over them as he taxis to the runway and he sees the taxiway lights out the windows. Few instructors can resist the temptation to, with the twist of a dial, turn a perfectly nice, clear day into a snowscape complete with icy taxiways. The terror is very real as the trainee watches his airplane slide slowly toward the ditch, and the anger can be just as real, when said instructor starts chortling in unrestrained glee while our man fights, every bit as hard as he would out on a real icy taxiway, to control the beast.

"Just our little way of teaching you some humility, Sport."

If the new hire is lucky, he will have the box all to himself, for at least the first few "flights." One student will get instruction on the second officer's panel, which is about all he will work for the next five to ten years, while another student "flies" the box; then they swap around. After about four more weeks of this, the box in the morning, more tapes and classes in the afternoon, and a lot of study at night, our birdmen are ready to hit the line on a real flight, although they're still not out of training. An instructor will accompany them on all flights for the first few weeks, until the new boy gets comfortable. Once on his own, the new engineer is required to inform his captain, on each flight, that he is still relatively inexperienced. He does not really have to do this. A captain can spot a new man a mile off: something to do with a shiny new uniform, bright new stripes and a brand new flight bag.

After meeting his captain, who determines the fuel load for this segment of the flight, our man heads for the airplane. There he will begin his preflight inspection and make sure all is ready, even though the machine has already been carefully inspected by a team of mechanics. Anything amiss will be brought to the captain's attention.

The new begins to wear off after the first year and, over the next few years the second officer (. . . or S/O) starts lusting after the first officer's (. . . F/O) seat. The F/O gets to fly, really fly, not just ride while the other guys have all of the fun. The S/O dutifully works his panel, monitors the systems, pre-flights airplane after airplane and watches the pilots do the flying. Over the years, he learns different techniques from different pilots. It is a helpless feeling to be strapped in the back seat, with no controls, watching someone else making the decisions.

Pilots, on the whole, live by a certain set of laws that permit no tampering: the laws of nature. If, for example, a pilot allows his airplane to get too slow, it is nature's law that decrees that the airplane must now stall and fall. There is no court of appeals that can delay that descent. No staying orders or picket lines protesting the unfairness of the laws can hold an airplane aloft when the laws have been broken. This is a basic foundation of a pilot's life and tends to carry over in his private life even when he is on the ground. He is basically going to be conservative, preferring to apply logic to his decisions rather than passion. This credo is true in everything, that is, until you begin to examine his need to fly.

Put as simply as possible, flying is what a pilot is, and everything else is what he or she does. There is a difference here. There are precious few humans whose lot in life is to be paid to do something that, given a choice, would be their first selection. Most people are never really given the choice in the first place. Thousands of people do whatever it is they do to earn their daily bread, then they go out and spend much of what they earn seeking flight. I cannot explain this addiction to flying that consumes the people who do it, nor will I even attempt to understand it myself. It is important that you know this fact and I am repeating an earlier statement, because you as a passenger want a man in the cockpit who chooses to be there, and does not dream of being elsewhere.

THE PROMOTION TO FIRST OFFICER

Our new hire is no longer new. His stripes are a bit dulled and his flight bag is no longer shiny. The older captains have been retiring, and the airline has been expanding. One very bright day, he sees the teletype. He is scheduled for training as F/O. First officer — a real pilot — no longer is he to be known as a "plumber," a "tire kicker" or as "Mr. Fixit." He is going to "get a hold of the big wheel, and make the houses get little."

He goes back to the training school and back through the same training that he had years ago. Only, this time, he will be teamed with a new captain. When he reaches the simulator, he will be in the right front seat, undergoing exactly the same training as the captain. At first, he will feel awkward, rusty at the controls, but the years of watching will help him overcome this. Soon the box will start to feel better and, as he progresses, the instructor will begin to throw everything but the kitchen sink at the new F/O, just as he has thrown it at the captain. Engine failures, hydraulic failures, low ceilings and thunderstorms are the norm in the box. Sweat pours off of him as he wrestles the airplane (he does not question that this is, in fact, an airplane and not a simulator) into the slot on a single engine, hydraulic failure approach to a 200 foot ceiling. There is very little chance that this would ever happen on the line, but to have done it, to have successfully landed out of the worst possible circumstances, does a lot for our man's confidence.

Walking back to the hotel, the captain may offer something like, "That was a doggone nice approach tonight. Let's go have a beer and celebrate."

"Yes Sir, Cap'n. This Bud is for the men that fly the BIG jets."

If the captain were to look down, he would notice that the new copilot was walking about six inches off the ground. He will soon come down to earth.

The first time that the new airman actually boards an airplane for the purpose of flight, it will be with passengers. Up until now, his sole experience at the controls has been in the box. Now it is for real, and you, gentle reader, may be one of those passengers. Not to worry because, on his left, the new copilot will have an instructor captain who will be keeping a very close eye on things — a very close eye, indeed. The first few landings may be a bit rough, more like arrivals, but it only takes a few of those to get the hang of it. Soon, our hero will be "slicking 'em on," just like a pro. Remember, he is not new to flying. He is just new to this airplane. More importantly, he will begin the process of forming judgments and making decisions, always at the captain's discretion, and learning the foundation of command. It is not a rapid process, nor is it an easy one. He will fly with some captains from whom he will learn a great deal, and others who could take a few lessons from him. At least it will seem that way. A cockpit is not a democracy. The captain may be right or he may be wrong, but he is always the captain.

THE COPILOT GAINS YEARS OF EXPERIENCE

From day one, the new copilot will fly every other leg of the day, only relinquishing control if the weather is below his minimums of 300 feet of cloud ceilings and ¾ mile visibility. During his years as second-in-command, he will actually fly, not ride, through everything his captains have ever seen. Stories will be exchanged at dinner in hotels all over the country. Techniques will be discussed (and sometimes simply cussed). Little tricks that do not appear in any Flight Operations Manual. This is for a very simple reason: someday, that old captain will bring his family out to the airport for a vacation trip and there will be a new captain in the left seat. The older man knows what kind of experience the younger man has had, because he has taught him. He can board the airplane and relax.

The years will pass and the new copilot will know, first hand, the old aviation adage that "flying is hours and hours of sheer boredom, sparked by moments of stark terror." Those moments are really not all that terrible, but they will seem that way to him, and he will learn from them. He will learn where not to stick his nose, like in a Florida thunderstorm. He will learn when to carry extra fuel, such as the night Memphis was reporting clear skies, but a temperature/dewpoint spread of only 1°, with no wind. When he arved, the world had turned to milk...fog so thick that you could get out and walk on it. He will learn these things, and a thousand more.

His logbook will show almost 10,000 flying hours, and from the very beginning he has flown every other leg of every flight. The captains have come to know and trust him, in good weather and bad.

THE NEW CAPTAIN

The years slip by, but so do the numbers—the seniority numbers that determine when our man can fly captain. From a standpoint of skill and judgment, he has been ready for a long time, but he must wait for the numbers. He begins to keep count. "Let's see, 15 retire in June and old Captain Blotz had a heart attack." (As badly as he wants to fly captain, he hates to get a number that way.) Then, at long last, after only 17 years, there it is on the bulletin board.

"BLOW, J. FROM: F/O ------- TO: CAPT B-727."

There will be general rejoicing in the Blow household tonight, and tomorrow he will visit his tailor. He will need a new uniform, one with four stripes and, while he is there, he might try on a new hat, one with all the chicken tracks on it.

Back to training. Captain Blow has flown the airplane in the other two seats, and he knows it pretty well, but he still crawls back into the books. This time the FAA will be along on the check ride, and they are legendary in their ability to ask questions that can trip up the best prepared student, so he studies harder than ever. Then he studies some more—charts and books and manuals that he never needed before.

THE TYPE-RATING PROCESS

Our new captain already has his Airline Transport Rating, his pilot's license. Now he must be "type rated," meaning that he must be trained and checked in each type of aircraft that he will fly for an airline. The licenses can be equated with college degrees. The commercial license is the bachelor's degree of the aviation world, while the Airline Transport Rating is the master's degree. The type rating is the Ph.D. and must be held by every captain in airline service. In addition, if our captain moves to a different airplane, he must again be type rated in the new bird.

As an F/O or S/O, he must return to the training school once a year for recurrent training, a sort of annual refresher course. He must spend about four hours in the box, rehearsing the failures and emergencies he never sees on the line. He must take a comprehensive physical examination each year.

The real training, however, has been out on the line, on your flight. He knows the cockpit of that airplane like you know the way to the office. He has probably made more takeoffs and landings than you have made that familiar trip. He knows the operation of one radar, seven radios and those critical seven instruments, before him, as well as the best home-maker knows her own microwave oven. A hundred different captains have shown him a hundred techniques for flying, and he has chosen his own. The F/O lands the airplane, in all kinds of weather, like a pro because he is a pro.

Now, as a captain, he will take two physicals, complete with EKG exams, and two checkrides each year. The airline also sends one of its instructor captains along with him, at least once a year. Nobody wants this guy to develop any bad habits along the way and, as a passenger, you certainly don't.

The type rating process consists of an oral examination, by the FAA, that can take up to 8 hours, and two simulator flights of four hours each. The FAA man will only comment when he wants to see a certain maneuver again, and he almost always does. It is his way of putting a little pressure on the trainee, and it does just that.

Back in the debriefing room, the "Fed" will unload with all the comments he has been saving back in the box. The would-have-been captain starts reflecting on a new career as a ditch digger, certain that with all the imperfections confronting him, his days as a pilot are over. Suddenly the Fed stops talking, signs the captain's ticket, and leaves the room. It is over, and a brand new captain has been born. Well, almost. There is the matter of flying the real airplane, and of learning how to "fly in reverse."

Up until this point, he has flown as F/O, using his right hand on the control wheel and his left hand on the throttles. He must now reverse that and fly from the other side of the airplane. It is a little clumsy at first, but he will soon master the change.

"Find me an old shirt, Honey. I'm on a trip tomorrow."

"Nonsense. For your first flight as captain, I will not have you leaving the house in an old shirt."

"Get me an old shirt. They are going to tear it off me

after the trip."

After that first flight, with an instructor captain now in the right seat, the instructor does indeed cut the back out of the captain's shirt, and hangs it on the wall. As each captain with whom our man has flown in years past passes by, he will scrawl his name and comments on the shirt tail near the large notation:

CAPT. JOE BLOW, FIRST FLIGHT DATED 10-5-84 — 17 YEARS, 4 MONTHS, 8 DAYS.

Later, Captain Blow will take that scrap of cloth home and put it in a place of honor.

THE LONG WAIT FOR SENIORITY

The journey has just begun however, and the new captain must pay some more dues. He has been paying dues since he first joined the airline.

When he was a brand new S/O, all those long years ago, he was on reserve, which meant that he never knew when he would be called for a flight. Usually, when a senior S/O called in sick or went on vacation, a reserve would be called for the trip. This wasn't terribly hard to take, when he was young. He had just started the best career a fellow could have and didn't have the money to go out a lot anyway. All his friends understood if they were also with the airline. They knew that a promise to join them for dinner in a few days always carried the unspoken, "if I don't get called." Non-airline people, who couldn't understand, quit calling about the second time they got stuck with a bunch of steaks, a hot barbecue grill and, suddenly, no company. Wives, with brand new babies, learned to cope alone. (Two of the writer's three children were delivered while he languished in some far away hotel.)

The months turned into years and, one fine day, the not-so-new-anymore S/O was awarded a "line of flying." He was finally off the reserve list.

The trip he would fly for the full month was, truly, a dog. A three day safari, he would check in before dawn the first two days and return just before midnight on the third day. During those three days, he would fly fifteen "legs" which included a takeoff and landing, and he would change airplanes a total of six times. This meant a complete preflight inspection at least twice each day.

It was a dog, but who cared. He is off reserve, and he

and his bride could make some plans. Well, almost.

The engines whined down, the main cabin door opened and the tension began to flow, almost visibly, from the crew. It had been a difficult trip, with bad weather everywhere, an air conditioning system that had a mind of its own and a cabin crew which constantly complained, "It's too hot back here. . .it's too cold back here. . .it's too hot. . ." No, it had not been your basic, real nice day, and for the exausted S/O Blow, things were just about to really go downhill.

An agent stuck his head into the cockpit, and read from a note:

"S/O Blow, you are to call Crew Schedule at extension. . ."

"WHAT? YOU'VE GOT TO BE KIDDING!"

"That's extension. . ."

"I KNOW THE DAMNED NUMBER. I WILL NEVER FORGET THAT DAMNED NUMBER FOR THE REST OF MY DAYS ON THIS EARTH! MY WIFE AND MY CHILDREN KNOW THAT DAMNED NUMBER, AND THAT DAMNED NUMBER WILL BE IMPLANTED IN THE GENES OF MY GRANDCHILDREN WHO WILL NOT BE BORN FOR AT LEAST TWENTY YEARS!"

By the time our man had delivered himself of this soliloquy, the agent had sought the relative calm of a hundred grumbling passengers. The captain and F/O glanced at each other knowingly and the captain observed, "Young fellow, you have just been drafted."

Drafted! For some reason, the regular S/O for the next day's flight to Albany could not make it. All of the reserves were busy with trips, or vacations, or for some other reason, could not cover the trip to Albany. As the junior line holder, who should get three days off, Joe got drafted to fly. It did not happen often, and as he continued to move up the ladder, it ceased to happen at all. The trips started to get better, and he could pretty much select the days he would fly and those that he would be off. Seniority is nice, but he was still not doing what he came to the airline to do. Fly.

When he checked out in the right seat as first officer, Joe went back to the bottom of a new list. First officer reserve, and he once again began the climb.

As a brand new captain, the whole process starts over

again. Reserve Captain Blow stays at home a lot, near the phone. He and his wife, having been through it all before, don't make many firm plans for a few years.

More years pass, better trips start to be available and he has long since become comfortable with the aging, but friendly, Boeing 727. The old girl has become as close to him as a member of his family. The kids are all in high school, and Joe enjoys being able to bid his trips so as to go see his boy play on the school football team, and help his daughter with her physics. (. . . I tell you, the kid will get a scholarship to M.I.T., at the rate she's going.) Soon, though, he will have to make another decision.

In addition to the Boeing 727, his airline operates the larger, more modern Boeing 767 and the majestic Boeing 747. In a few more years he will be in the numbers to fly the 767, with the attendant raise in pay. But that also means that he would have to go through the type rating process again and, once rated, he would be back on the bottom of another seniority list. Back on reserve again.

It will be this way until the end of his career with the airline: move up to the larger airplanes and make more money, or stay with the lower paying, older airplane, but have a more normal home life. He could wait until it would be possible to be a line holder on the intermediate airplane but, by that time, he could possibly be in the numbers for the biggie, the 747. Then again, back to reserve, at an age where reserve is a real posterior pain.

THE STRESS OF THE FLYING GAME

Every pilot will go through a career, very much like the one described on these pages. The seniority number, his place in line, will control virtually his entire life. The good life is always just around the corner and, with it, comes the bad. All along the way is the semi-annual physical, which is pressure of a very particular kind. You could feel fine as you waltz into the doctor's office, and one lead on the EKG machine could squiggle the wrong way and it's all over. You are suddenly looking for another way to make a living, because pilots with heart problems are not in demand at all. And a grounded pilot is rarely very good at anything else, and never happy again.

There is stress in the flying game as there is in no other. There are a few nights each year when you study the radar

✈

intently, knowing that the weather, the storms it is showing, will not go away, and they are very, very close to the airport. You know that tonight you will earn every dime that you will ever make. You fervently wish that the crosswinds were not quite so violent, and that the airplane that landed before you had not made the comment about the braking action on the runway being poor. Airplanes never have problems on clear, bright days...always on dark, stormy nights. (My "how-to-write-a-book" book says to never use that phrase, "a dark, stormy night." The author of that book never flew an airplane on such a night.) It is on nights like this that one would happily trade every penny of that salary just to be somewhere else, but in an airliner there may not be a somewhere else. The crew will reach back into their bag of tricks, their thousands of hours of experience and training and then they will get the job done, or will have the judgment to turn away and go to a more hospitable airport.

As a passenger, do not get too cross with the captain who realizes that he may not have the skills to reach your blizzard-swept destination. Be grateful that he has the judgment, and the honesty, to recognize his limitations.

THE LIGHTER SIDE OF AIRLINE FLYING

None of this prevents most pilots from developing a healthy sense of humor. This may trouble a few who actually believe the cockpit scenes as depicted by the movies, with pilots sitting straight, with (for heaven's sake) their headsets clamped over their caps, all deadly serious, all business and usually sawing earnestly away on the steering wheel. These same people believe that famous surgeons never crack a black joke in the operating room and that lawyers don't have an occasional laugh at the misfortunes of their clients. A person who plods along through life, not enjoying his own calling very much and not expecting anyone else to enjoy theirs, is mistaken. These little gray people are to be pitied.

Whole books have been written about the lighter side of airline flying and some of the fabled stories are actually true. All of them provide crews with much merriment which, in fact, can ease a lot of strain. One captain carries a large pair of fuzzy dice to hang momentarily from the windshield wiper switch, and another drapes a pair of baby shoes from the same switch. A captain, now retired, used to carry a rubber chicken of the sort that one gets in a novelty shop, with a bit of twine around its scrawny neck. Approaching the gate, our man would open his window and hang the chicken outside for the mechanics to see as he came to a halt.

"What is that, Charlie?" the mechanic would shout up to the cockpit, "Bird Strike?"

"Yeah," the captain would reply, "We got two of 'em. Cooked one for lunch, and saved the other one for you guys."

This writer was the recipient of a well planned, and beautifully executed bit of humor by a favorite flight attendant.

We had completed a perfectly normal flight, early in my career as a new captain, a full fifteen years from retirement. We parked at the gate and turned off the seat-belt sign as a signal for the passengers to get up.

Suddenly hands started appearing in the cockpit and there were congratulations. Many, many congratulations.

"Way to go, captain...congratulations...nice job..."

"What in the world is this all about," I wondered. "The landing was good, but not THAT good, just normal."

When one older gentleman confided, as he shook my hand vigorously, "Don't believe everything you hear, Captain, you are going to love it."

I hung on to his hand, "What am I going to enjoy? What am I not supposed to believe?"

"Don't let it get you down, Captain, retirement is really great."

"Retirement," I roared. "I'm nowhere near..." Then I looked past the gentleman and saw the dazzling smiles of the two flight attendants, tears of laughter rolling down their cheeks.

They had made a convincing announcement, as we approached Washington, that this was to be my last landing. After this one, I would be retiring after so many years with the airline. They had encouraged the passengers to offer their congratulations as they left the airplane. All 75 people aboard agreed that this would be a nice thing to do, and proceeded to do so with enthusiasm.

That was ten years ago and I still wonder what I might do to...well, sort of even the score. Anne and Casey are both still flying and some day, on some flight...!

Simple-minded humor, perhaps. But it also served a

very useful purpose, loosening up a tight crew near the end of a long day's flying. Nothing can return one's perspective faster than a smile or a good laugh. Nothing can sweep away the strain and mental cobwebs as quickly and return a crew to the alertness that they need for that last leg home.

SCENARIO: THE CAPTAIN'S LAST FLIGHT

Finally, the last flight...the last landing, and all those years on reserve, all the schools and physicals, the nights with crummy weather and the hours of glorious boredom are going to be behind him after one more landing.

Let's call him Captain Smith and put him in the left seat of a huge, heavy Lockheed L-1011 coming from San Juan to Miami. The night is clear and smooth and the airplane is perfect. It was really the F/O's turn to fly that last leg, but there was never any question, in anybody's mind, as to who would really fly it. It was Captain Smith's last trip. His family, and a few friends, were waiting at the gate in Miami with some champagne and a sign to hang around his neck: "JUST RETIRED." He would not even sip the champagne. For 32 years he had never had a drink while in uniform and saw no reason to start now and, besides, there would be a number of passengers nearby. "I don't want them to get the wrong idea." But he would wear the sign and hear the congratulations of his friends, and he would go home.

But first, there was that last landing. One has dark fantasies about the last landing. The gear won't come down, or a tire will blow, or a hundred other things that could happen will happen. Fate is not going to let him end a career of 32 years and 18,000 flying hours without tossing him one last challenge. Tonight, however, fate has the evening off, and all goes smoothly for Captain Smith, his crew and 287 passengers. The gear does come down, and three blessed green lights indicate that it is locked. The weather stays clear, the wind almost calm and Captain Smith settles into the same approach pattern he had flown more than 10,000 times before.

The runway lights began to grow. In his windshield, he could see the large, white painted runway numbers rushing to meet him at 150 miles per hour.

THUMP...THUMP, and they were down...only... what's this? The passengers were startled to feel themselves pressed back in their seats as the engines accelerated back to full power and the huge machine took flight again.

After they had re-entered the traffic pattern, Captain Smith, who had never done an irrational thing in his life, picked up the cabin microphone and addressed his apprehensive passengers.

"FOLKS, THIS IS CAPTAIN SMITH. I WANT TO APOLOGIZE IF YOU WERE STARTLED AT OUR PULL UP, BACK IN MIAMI, AND I WANT TO SAY I AM SORRY FOR THE EXTRA FEW MINUTES OF FLYING. YOU SEE, THIS IS MY LAST FLIGHT BEFORE MY RETIREMENT, AND I WANTED MY LAST LANDING TO BE A REAL GOOD ONE. THE LANDING IN MIAMI WAS A GOOD ONE...BUT NOT GOOD ENOUGH. I'D LIKE TO GO BACK OUT AND GET IT RIGHT. THANKS FOR YOUR PATIENCE."

The next landing, five minutes later, was a real "grease job" and Captain Smith was able to, with the cheers of his passengers and the astonishment of his crew, leave the airport a happy man. Many things could have happened on that extra little flight, but they didn't. Fate was positively beaming on Captain Smith that night. Later, when a friend asked if he had considered the legality of his actions, he replied with a nervous smile, "What are they going to do ...ground me?"

Within a few hours of his last landing, he was greeting his sixtieth birthday, and his airline transport rating was automatically revoked by an unthinking computer. A quick press of a "delete" key by an uncaring operator, the lightning fast travel of a few millivolts, and Captain Smith's name vanished from a vast memory data base. He was, in that micro-second, officially retired.

His name was not Smith, but everything else about the story you have just read was true.

THE FLIGHT ATTENDANT

So far we have concentrated our little study of the crew on the pilots; however, the fact is that the pilots of any given airline make up only a small percentage of the total number of employees of the company. It is the pilot who must deliver the product of that company — safe, comfortable air transportation. However, the average passenger is going to form his impressions of the airline and, to a large

➤

extent, his desire to accept or reject its service in the future, by the people he meets in the cabin: the flight attendants. These are the representatives of the airline whom the passenger spends most of his time observing.

Flight attendants, formerly known as stewardesses, hostesses, and a few other descriptions, have suffered for a long time under the cloud of a few sensationalist pocket books of years past. The well-known *Coffee, Tea or Me* painted a pretty spicy picture of life aloft, and abed, and was widely read and just as widely believed. A spicy picture, indeed, and grossly inaccurate and unfair to the young men and women who had to wade through the snide comments, the innuendoes and propositions which followed that publication and a few others like it. Perhaps the book accurately reflected life as the authors saw and, possibly, lived it, but it gave the vast majority of flight attendants a terrible cross to bear. It is said that nothing sells books as well as does sex, sex and more sex. I have far too much respect for these young people to be able to do that.

There was a time when airlines hired young women more for their ability to fill a blouse than a coffee cup, and the real purpose of a flight attendant was forgotten in the shuffle or jiggle. A few such airlines dressed their girls in little costumes (very little) that, with the help of the young lady herself, were designed to inflame the young businessman and make him vow never to fly the competition, ". . .'cause their skirts are too long." To a certain extent, the tactic must have worked, because a stewardess' career was usually a short one, about two years. Then she married one of the stunned young passengers and faded into the suburban sunset.

Thankfully, those years are behind the industry, and the airlines have long recognized the virtue of brains over breast. A winning personality is far more important than any physical quality, or lack of same. Unfortunately, deregulation threatens to change the airlines' search for quality people to a quest for those who will accept the lowest rate of pay.

What you, the passenger, will see on a normal flight is only one reason that the flight attendant is aboard. The meal and beverage services are vitally important to the airline and the image that they want you to carry away after your flight. Long hours are spent designing procedures for meal service. The actions of each member of the cabin staff are literally choreographed by dining services personnel, then refined by the flight attendants themselves, out on the line. If you don't believe this, just watch carefully the next time you are scheduled to have dinner aboard a hour and a half flight. What you will witness will put to rest a few myths.

DISPELLING THE MYTHS
ABOUT FLIGHT ATTENDANTS

If you were to expect to develop one of those inflight romances that you may have read about, you had better be one very fast talker, because you have about forty seconds in which to deliver your pitch. I'm not about to say that this kind of thing never happens. Of course it does, but with no more frequency than, say, a visitor striking up a friendship with a nurse in a hospital or a salesman with a secretary.

Another myth is that of the infamous crew parties at layover hotels. There are several reasons that this sort of thing simply does not happen.

The first is that most of these young men and women are happily married, have families and have little desire to fool around on the side.

The second is that, after a day of serving meals, beverages, warming milk for infants, taking care of the occasional case of airsickness or drunkeness, one can rarely turn one's attention to social adventure. A hot tub of water and a soft pillow are much to be preferred.

Third, at least on the larger airlines, the cockpit crew will fly with several cabin crews in a day's work. The reason for this is that rates of pay differ as well as the number of hours a crewmember can work each day. A flight attendant is allowed to work a few more minutes each day than can a pilot, and the scheduling computers have an eye for these small differences that can translate to large differences at year's end. An example:

On a typical day's flying, my cockpit crew and I may fly from Miami to Houston with a fresh Miami-based cabin crew. In Houston, we will leave the airplane which, with the cabin crew, will continue on to Los Angeles. We pick up a new airplane, with an Atlanta cabin crew, for a flight to Atlanta. Arriving in Atlanta, the cabin crew will go

✈

home. They have been up all night flying the "Late Show" from San Francisco, and we will pick up another New York-based crew for our flight to Boston. We will layover in Boston, and the airplane and cabin crew will fly to Miami. Not much opportunity for the well-known meaningful relationship here.

In fact, the contract with most hotels in which airline crews layover requires that a quiet floor be provided for crews, whose only interest in a hotel is how much sleep they can get. Let the hotel assign one of the rooms as a hospitality suite for a bunch of loud-mouthed drunks on a convention and, in very short order, the hotel will lose the airline's business. This has happened on occasion.

FLIGHT ATTENDANTS ENSURE YOUR SAFETY

None of this has really approached the real reason for the flight attendants' presence on board. Their personalities and the service that they provide are what you see, but what you don't see is the real reason that they are there, and that is for your safety. Never, ever forget that.

Federal Air Regulations require one flight attendant for each 49 seats aboard an airplane. Seats, not passengers. If a flight attendant, part of a crew of two flight attendants on a 90 passenger airplane, were to fall ill on a layover, the airplane cannot be dispatched with even one passenger until a replacement can be provided. It has happened.

When this ruling first came into being, the captain of an airplane, with seats for 50, found himself in Charleston, South Carolina, with one sick flight attendant and one too many seats. Having seen to the girl's medical needs in a local hospital, he saw no further need for delay. Yet it was not legal to fly his airplane with only the remaining flight attendant, so he set to scratching his head and came up with the only answer available. Take out a seat. He grabbed a couple of wrenches from the back of an agent's car (there were no mechanics in Charleston at that time), unbolted a pair of seats, stored them in the baggage compartment and, happily and legally, left right on schedule with 35 passengers aboard—and one flight attendant. The ill flight attendant and the seats were replaced at his next stop in Atlanta.

During their initial training, these young men and women are given exaustive training on the safety features and equipment of each airplane that the line operates. They spend many hours on the subjects of First Aid, Evacuation, Ditching and other emergency procedures. All of this training is given by instructors, carefully selected by the airline from veteran flight attendants with years of experience, and under the watchful eyes of the FAA.

Once on the line, the new flight attendant will bid her trips just as the pilots do, on a basis of seniority, of which she has little. She will fly the dog trips for several years, with no time for a real social life.

"Yes, Bill, I would love to have dinner with you, if I'm in town."

"What do you mean, if you are in town? Either you want to go out with me, or you don't."

"I'll tell you what, Bill, you keep in touch, O.K.?" (You are a nice enough guy, Bill, but you have to learn that my schedule is not the same as someone working 9 to 5 with every weekend off.)

SCENARIO: A DAY IN THE LIFE OF A FLIGHT ATTENDANT

I have already mentioned that the carry-on baggage problem is the largest that the flight attendant must suffer. Add to that the matter of carry on pets. Most airlines will allow one dog or one cat in each cabin (First Class or Coach) in an approved carrier that will fit underneath the passenger's seat. The animal must remain in the carrier throughout the flight.

There are people who cannot tolerate the idea that their darling little Fifi is to be imprisoned in a stupid box for two whole hours. So, once airborne, the little critter is uncrated and allowed to roam.

It was on one such occasion that justice finally triumphed.

Halfway between Newark and Daytona Beach, the flight attendant came up to the cockpit and wearily announced that she had just about "had it up to here with that damned woman and her accursed little doggie."

"The passengers are really complaining about the yapping, and the damned dog is running around marking his territory all over the place."

"Did you ask her to put the dog back in the box?" the captain asked.

"About a dozen times, till she started cursing me."

The captain then went back to see if he could cite the

regulations and talk some reason to the lady. He soon returned with a complexion rather resembling that of a cooked beet.

After about a ten minute monologue, which I dared not interrupt, he finally said, "She said her dog had as much right as anyone else in the airplane, and would not be put in the box, and if I did not like it I could land and put her off. She knew that I would not delay the rest of the passengers for that."

At Daytona Beach, we watched in silent fury as the woman, the box in one hand and the still barking pooch in the other, paraded arrogantly by the cockpit and off the airplane. We then returned to Newark.

A week later, we landed at Daytona Beach on the same trip. We were about a half-hour late and the passengers were already lined up for their journey to New Jersey. As we walked past them, our eyes locked like radar on the most beautiful sight we had seen in days.

All 190 pounds of her, with her huge straw beach hat, her fuchsia muumuu, and her puppy in one hand, the carrier in the other.

"You see her, don't you Neil?"

"Yep... it's almost too good to be true."

We finished filling out our flight papers and returned to the airplane. The passengers were already on board, but over on a baggage cart was an animal carrier complete with a very disgruntled poodle.

"I guess she recognized us, too."

"Yep."

Halfway to Newark, the flight attendant came up.

"You guys know who's back there, don't you?"

"Yep... any trouble?"

"No, she's very quiet."

"Good... take her a drink and tell her Captain's compliments."

"How lovely," smiled the young lady as she took her leave.

OTHER AIRLINE PERSONNEL

There are a lot more people who work very hard, first to get you to buy a ticket on their airline, then to check you in at the airport. Shop workers overhaul airplane parts and mechanics install them. Electronics and instrument shops overhaul critical equipment that cannot fail and doesn't. Crew schedulers try to find pilots and flight attendants to fill each crewmember seat while financial beancounters insist that there are too many crewmembers on the payroll and resist hiring. Traffic planning experts, meanwhile, are adding new routes and marketing wizards are selling charter flights. Computer services are frantically trying to keep up with the daily changes in fares and schedules.

Most of this chapter has been devoted to those who are most directly, most immediately, involved in your safety. The flight crews. To give fair and equal treatment to all of the people who are concerned with your flight would be all but impossible. Not only do the space limitations of this book make that impossible, but my own knowlege of their tasks is limited. I started my career in aviation as a mechanic, but that was thirty five years ago. I remember the misery of changing a huge tire in the middle of a Maine blizzard, but I could not hold a wrench with today's mechanic. These people can read a complicated circuit diagram like I read a newspaper. They are good and the highest compliment I can pay them is the trust I place in their work.

I cannot offer enough praise to the flight crew schedulers who often have to fill cockpits with nonexisistent pilots. They are on the receiving end of a lot of verbal abuse when they have to call some senior captain out during the captain's days off. Imagine their feelings when they have to call someone and say, "We are going to have to cancel flight 123 to Boston. We just don't have a captain for the trip." To cancel a flight is an extremely serious thing to do.

No, I could never do all of these folks justice. You can believe that they are a special breed of people. Every one of them knows what rides on their performance: your safety and comfort.

Everyone working for an airline, from the corporate officers to the aircraft cleaners, throbs with human energy throughout the entire day and all of this energy is focused on one man saying to another, over a scratchy interphone connection:

"Captain, if your doorlights are out and your brakes are set, you are cleared to start engines...have a nice flight."

CHAPTER 4

THE AIRPLANE

We are going to start getting a little technical here, and if you are the sort of person who flatly rejects the fact that machines have been of benefit to mankind, who refuses to even consider the workings of a flashlight bulb, and believes that the human race can be saved only by a total rejection of any technology that you don't understand, then you should move along to another chapter. But, before you do, I would like to suggest to you that the modern airliner is not really as complicated as it would first appear. It is not, for example, any more complicated than the modern automobile. By the nature of its task, the airliner had better not be as complex as the new automobile, simply because, when an airliner starts developing troubles, one can't ease over to the side of the road and call AAA.

"C'mon," you say, "You're telling me that my Oldsmobile is more complicated than a 727?"

That is exactly what I am telling you. Your new Olds has a rather sophisticated electronic ignition system and perhaps an electronic fuel injection system as well. The 727 has a simple ignition system, with no distributor, to help get the engines started. Then you turn the ignition off, as the engine no longer needs it to keep running. The device that meters the fuel to the engine is a simple, but very precise, mechanical device. The engine in your Olds has hundreds of moving parts that must whirl and jiggle in perfect harmony...rubbing, scuffing and otherwise torturing one another. One jet engine, as installed on the 727, has only two moving parts and they only whirl on well-oiled bearings.

The complexity, or apparent complexity, of the airliner lies in the fact that there is a lot more of it than there is to your Olds. There are a lot of simple systems...three engines, for example, instead of only one.

But, I'm getting ahead of myself so, if you are still with me, let's go back to basics.

THE WING IS WHAT COUNTS

We cannot get much more basic than the wing, and yet without it, there would be no airplane, just a very fast bus.

Everyone has seen the old newsreel clips of man's early attempts to fly and, for the most part, those early "bird-men" had the right idea. They had seen the birds fly, knew that the long, graceful wings of the bird held the secret, and dreamed up all sorts of ways of imitating said bird. For a long time, the inventors thought that it should be sufficient to create appendages that only looked like those of the bird, so they would strap all manner of wings to their bodies, go up on the barn and demonstrate the art of falling.

It finally occurred to someone that the secret was two-fold. The wing had to be shaped a certain way and there had to be a continuous flow of air over the surface. These two things, shape and airflow, could then make use of nat-ural law. Without using a lot of physics-ese, the law states that if you accelerate air over a surface the pressure of the air will decrease as the air is forced to move faster over the surface. Add a curve to the top of the surface while leaving the bottom flat, and the air must go even faster over the top of the surface than it does over the bottom. The pressure of the air moving over the curved, upper surface will be lower than that of the relatively slower air passing over the bot-tom surface. The whole surface will want to rise. Get the air moving fast enough and the surface will rise; faster still and the surface will lift a load, such as an airplane full of people.

The wing is the whole show, and virtually everything else on the machine is dedicated to keeping air moving in an orderly manner over that surface.

The engines are tacked on merely to push the wing through the air fast enough to keep it lifting its load.

However, simply lifting the load is not quite enough. To do the work of an airplane, you must be able to control the wing...make it go up and down and turn. You do this by changing the angle at which the wing attacks the air.

You demonstrated this to yourself years ago, when you would stick your hand out of the car window (to the dismay of your mother) and experiment by changing the angle of

✈

your hand and feeling your hand fly up and down. You probably found that just the right angle would allow your hand to support the weight of your arm, a nice balance.

If the wing is really the only thing that counts, what are all those little wings back on the tail? All they do is help control the angle of attack of the wing. If the elevator, the horizontal tail surface, forces the tail down a bit the angle of the wing will increase and up we go. The rudder on a jet, the vertical fin, keeps the airplane pointed in a given direction and helps keep the machine straight in the event an engine should fail, which would cause more engine thrust on one side than the other.

That's about all there is to an airplane. If the engines push the wing along fast enough, the wing will lift everything up. Simple!

THE IMPORTANCE OF WING FLEX

This is as good a place as any to explain something that causes all sorts of anxiety among infrequent fliers. Wing flex. You are zipping along through the clouds and you notice that the wing is literally flapping up and down. It is bending and you do not particularly like watching it do so.

Without devoting an entire chapter to the construction of the wing, accept that the wing is carefully designed to flex rather than to remain rigid. In this way, gust loads are distributed to, and absorbed by, the entire airplane instead of a small, localized, part of it. Since the wing is the part of the airplane that is subjected to these gust loads, it is better to have it "flow along" with sudden changes in lifting forces rather than transmit these forces to the body, or fuselage. Just as the flexible willow tree will withstand greater wind forces than the mighty, but more rigid, oak, so too will a flexible wing withstand more gust loads than the stiff wing.

The last airplane to have a stiff wing design was the Lockheed Electra, whose entire wing was machined from huge, solid billets of aluminum. This produced a very strong, but inflexible wing. Those who flew the Electra loved its flying characteristics—until they encountered choppy air. Then they described it as the original "Rough Rider." I had the pleasure of spending just over a year in the cockpit of this wonderful airplane. At least it was a pleasure until, early one morning, I encountered a small rainshower with its attendant moderate turbulence.

The cockpit of any airplane is on the end of a long moment arm, just like the end of a spring-board. If you were to shake the fixed end of a spring-board, all sorts of gyrations would occur on the free end. So it was with the Electra. The crew is on the end of a springboard that is being vigorously shaken by the inflexible wing. That, dear reader, was a real thrill ride with our heads flopping around so severely that it was impossible to read the instruments. The ride back in the cabin was not much smoother.

There are some things that, in the course of life, one must accept on faith even though one's senses say otherwise. Accept that the flexible wing is much stronger than the rigid wing. You may accept, as simple fact, that only one airplane, with the modern flexible wing design, has ever been lost to structural failure and that one, a Boeing 707, was inadvertantly flown into the living heart of what is called, a "mature" thunderstorm. A big, boiling, black-as-night thunderstorm. Even then, it was estimated by crash investigation experts, that the airplane would have survived had the crew not attempted to fight for control, adding unbearable stresses to those of the storm.

It has been proven, time and time again, that the basic structure of the jet that you will fly is incredibly strong. Airplanes have fallen thousands of feet, literally out of control, subjected to stresses far beyond those for which the machine was designed, and have survived. The airplanes were hurt, yes. The passengers were frightened, yes, but they, and the airplane that bore them, survived.

So much for wing flex. We were in the process of designing ourselves an airplane, so let us return to that task.

Of course, just having a wing isn't quite enough. You have to do something with it. You need to have something to keep the tail hooked up to the wing and a place to hang the engines. Build a nice long platform and place some seats on it. *Voilà!* You have yourself an airplane: a drafty one, but an airplane nonetheless. Now, enclose the seats, heat the inside, put in some ovens for meals and a small bar.

There are airliners flying today that are very little more than that described above. An airframe, a few engines and a place for the passengers to sit.

The jets are a little more complex, and for a very good reason.

EVERY SYSTEM HAS A BACKUP SYSTEM

I promised, early in the book, that I would give you a one word reason that airline travel is as safe and reliable as it is.

That word is REDUNDANCY: 1. Exceeding what is necessary or natural. 2. Needlessly repetitive.

Nothing is ever done on an airplane in singular. Every system has a backup system. If the system in question is even remotely critical, there is a backup to back up the backup. The more critical the system, the more backups.

Example: The hydraulic system on the Boeing 727 is a pretty critical system. It provides the muscle to raise and lower the landing gear, operate the flaps and, most importantly, it powers the flight control boost system. So we design a complex, but basically simple hydraulic system.

System A. The main hydraulic system is powered by two high capacity pumps, driven by two of the airplane's three engines. If any one engine, or any one pump, were to fail, the system is still fully powered. This is the first stage of redundancy. What if (remember that phrase?) a leak developed in the system itself and you lost all of the fluid from system A?

System B. A totally separate system. In no way connected to system A, system B is powered by two electrically driven pumps. Even though system B is not physically connected to system A, it powers half of each important flight control. The loss of either system B pump would have little effect on the systems operation, but what if you lost both systems A and B? Damned little chance of that ever happening, but what if?

Standby hydraulic system. A third electrical hydraulic pump, powered by an emergency electrical system, will partially power the most critical flight controls and lower the flaps. The landing gear can be lowered simply by manually unlatching it and allowing it to fall down of its own weight. The other flight control boost packages are designed so that, with the complete loss of all hydraulic power, they will automatically revert to manual operation. The airplane will be very difficult and sluggish to fly, but it can be flown. Remember, the engines are still running, pushing the wing through the air and that's flying.

During training, in the simulator, every pilot is given a failure of two engines (the ones driving the hydraulic pumps) and the total loss of system B. He is flying a crippled airplane with only one operating engine, is shown an airport and told to get her down. If he does not, he is allowed to experience the not very pleasant results, then he is taken out and allowed to do the whole scene all over again. As I have said before, the simulator is extremely realistic and the pilot tries very hard to get it right the first time. To the author's knowledge, this sort of thing has never happened to a real airplane, but what if. . . ?

The hydraulic system, for all its importance, is not the most critical system on the airplane. The electrical system has that honor because it powers the flight instruments and the flight instruments must, repeat, must remain powered. Let's take a look at the instruments, all of them, and that will lead us to the all important electrical system.

THE INSTRUMENTS IN THE COCKPIT

The single most repeated comment made by passengers who visit the cockpit and are confronted by the confusion of instruments, lights and switches, is, "Wow, how do you keep up with all this stuff?" The most honest answer we could give would be, "We don't."

Fully 90% of all those gadgets are of the "set it and forget it" variety. Once the switches for a certain system have been set, they probably won't have to be changed again for the entire flight. There are switches that need to be changed during the flight, but only when there is time to work slowly and deliberately. When I get a copilot or engineer who likes to show how fast he can crossfeed the fuel tanks or activate some other system, I start getting very nervous and, after a chat, he slows down. There is virtually nothing that needs doing in a real hurry. Get in too big a hurry and the chances are strong that you will do the wrong thing, hit the wrong switch, and just compound your problems. All of the instruments on the second officer's panel, the large panel along the right wall of the cockpit, are for informational purposes. They monitor the operation of several systems, but are of no immediate interest to the two pilots who are flying the airplane.

Up on the front panel, the instruments are a little more critical, but still, neither of the pilots is compelled to watch all of them all of the time.

Let's look at the three parts of the front panel. On the

left and right sides of this panel are the flight instruments, which absorb 90% of each pilot's attention. They are simply duplications of each other; therefore, each pilot has a full, independent set of flight instruments directly in front of him.

The center of this large panel contains the engine operating instruments. They are near the pilot's field of vision because they are frequently used to set or change the power of the engines whenever that is necessary. However, once the power has been adjusted, the pilot returns his attention to the flight instruments. These are the most essential items on the entire airplane, since they show the attitude of the ship, its speed, altitude and direction of flight. They also show the course to be flown and the airplane's position in relation to that course. These instruments must always give the proper information for the airplane to be flown safely; hence, they can be powered in a variety of ways. We are talking real redundancy here.

THE ELECTRICAL SYSTEMS

The electrical system powers the flight instrument groups. Actually, it is not really accurate to call it one electrical system, since there are six of them. In view of the fact that you, friend reader, are not going to be required to build a 727, to fly one, or even to take a test after reading this, I will simplify the electrical system as well as I can. The point I continue to make is that all of these systems are designed, by some very clever engineers, to be as failsafe as possible. After all, we are carrying a very precious cargo: real live people.

Each of the three engines drive a powerful generator. Each generator can carry the entire electrical load of the airplane without even breathing hard. Each generator powers its own electrical "bus," which is simply a way of saying that there are certain circuits assigned to each generator. If one, or two generators should fail, the remaining generator can handily power all of the buses by tying them all together. We already have some pretty serious redundancy going for us and we haven't even started yet.

The most critical items on the airplane are the captain's flight instruments, so we create a special bus, just for them and devise a way in which they can always be powered. Logically, we call this the "essential" bus.

The essential power bus is not simply powered by any of the other buses, but is given power directly from any generator on the airplane. Therefore, if a coffee maker were to short out bus #3, while the essential power were being drawn from generator #3, the bus might be lost (if, that is, the circuit breaker for the coffee maker didn't trip first) but the generator would still continue to power the essential bus. What if, you ask, the generator itself were to fail?

The essential bus would automatically be reassigned to another generator that was still producing power. If the automatic transfer system were to fail, the task can be done manually in about two seconds, restoring essential power.

By now, we have redundancy all the way up to our eyeballs, and there is still more. There is emergency standby power bus that can power the captain's most critical flight instruments, directly from the airplane's battery, for long enough to get the airplane down.

"What if..." Jeez, friend, haven't you had enough? Well, there is still one last back up, to help keep the wings level in the event that everything else went "toes up" (slang for inoperative). There is a separate, self-powered artificial horizon instrument that can allow a pilot to get out of the clouds and fly by "eyeball" without any instruments at all. It will not be a tidy approach, but remember, as long as the engines are still pushing that wing through the air and the pilot can see where he's going, the airplane can be flown and successfully landed. Remember, also, that the engines require no electrical power to operate.

For such a complete loss of electrical power to occur, there would have to be a massive electrical fire which the crew was ignoring. Crews are very sensitive to funny smells, and do not overlook something that smells electrical.

SCENARIO: AN ELECTRICAL FIRE

Remember Capt. C? He is our resident "bad luck Charlie" who feared thunderstorms. He wasn't all that crazy about the thought of inflight fires either. One dark, stormy night (there I go again, but like I said, it's my book) ol' Capt. C was blasting along through the ozone, dodging thunderstorms, when suddenly the hair stood up on the nape of his neck.

"I smell something," said C.

"It wasn't me," protested the copilot.

"Me either," offered the S/O.

"Not that," C pondered, "But somethin' almost — JEEZ, WE GOT A DAMNED ELECTRICAL FIRE."

With that, the crew hurried into the initial responses to an electrical fire, which include assuring that the captain's flight instruments would be powered, then shutting off all other systems. Along with all the cabin lights and many of the systems not considered critical to flight, Capt. C lost that item that he considered most essential to life itself, his weather radar.

"JEEZ, GIMME BACK MY RADAR," howled C.

The S/O began slowly to restore the systems to service, starting with the bus that would power the radar, and the smell disappeared. Encouraged, he restored more systems until the airplane was fully powered.

The senior flight attendant, who had dutifully remained out of the cockpit during what she accurately perceived to be an emergency, now came forward and asked just what in the world was going on.

"We had a damned electrical fire. Didn't you smell it?"

"All I smelled was burning broccoli," was her answer.

"Broccoli?"

"Broccoli...must have fallen off of a tray in one of the ovens...really stinks, doesn't it!"

The conversation that then ensued will go unreported. However, from that day forward, the flight attendants were puzzled by the sight of one of the line's captains checking behind the ovens on each flight, looking for broccoli.

No, one does not ignore unusual smells, or anything else, aboard an airplane and, with years of experience, crews learn to identify smells.

In this same vein, it is customary for the flight attendants to advise the captain when their cabin service has been completed. On the McDonald Douglas DC-9, however, this is not necessary. The galley is right behind the cockpit and, at the conclusion of service, the flight attendants are inclined to want to freshen up a bit, with about a quart of various perfumes.

When the air in the cockpit turns a lovely blue, the pilots know that service is done.

OTHER BACKUP SYSTEMS

There are more systems aboard, air conditioning, pressurization, pneumatic, fire and overheat detection and oxygen, to name a few. It should suffice to say that all of them enjoy the same protections and...well, that one word says it best, redundancy. Even the light sockets that indicate that the landing gear is down and locked have two bulbs each.

There is, also, a red light, with two bulbs, that will shine menacingly if the landing gear is not down and locked. The green lights can be dimmed at night, to prevent distracting glare. The red warning lights cannot be dimmed. When one comes on, the engineers want you to notice it, so they put another little warning circuit on the landing gear. If you pull the throttles back in preparation for landing, and the landing gear is not down and locked, a horn will blow in the cockpit. There is another horn that will toot if you advance the throttles for takeoff, when three critical controls are not in the appropriate position. The elevator trim tabs must be in the "takeoff range," the speedbrake handle must be in its full forward (speedbrakes retracted) position and the wing flaps must be in the takeoff position.

Other warnings include a sort of a berserk "cricket" that sounds if you exceed the maximum speed of the airplane and a stall warning system (two of the little devils, actually) that will make a pilot gray before his time. A device literally starts shaking the control wheel rapidly and a horn, of the size and tonal quality of those installed on diesel locomotives, will blast one out of the whatever stupor has allowed the airplane to get too slow. This horn is installed on the McDonald Douglas DC-9 but not on the Boeing 727. If, in the 727, the "stick shakers" do not get the pilot's attention, the S/O will start yelling as loud as any horn.

Very few pilots have ever heard the stall warning activate during actual flight and, of those few, none has ever heard it twice.

A big doorbell will ring if the fire detection system should detect a fire in one of the engines. This bell will ring occasionally, but only because of the very sensitive nature of the detection circuit. False warnings are common but are still treated as actual fires.

Mark this down in your little confidence book: in over twenty years service of thousands of the engines installed on

➤

your Boeing 727, 737 or McDonald Douglas DC-9, there has never been a case of one of these engines actually catching fire. (One accident has been blamed on an "engine fire"; however, it is suspected that the engine exploded and sent fragments into the fuel tank which caused the fire.)

There was a saying that originated among pilots back in World War II: "In God we trust...with Pratt and Whitney we fly."

The engines installed on your Boeing 727 and the other two airplanes noted above are Pratt and Whitney JT-8D engines. They are among the most reliable mechanical devices ever conceived by man, and the simplest. This fact provides much comfort to those who must fly these engines and depend on them, day after day after month after year. A pilot can develop a real affection for the works of Mr. P and Mr. W, when said pilot has been propelled over millions of miles on the invisible thrust of these engines.

THE JET ENGINE

"Suck, Squeeze, Burn and Blow." With this principle, and only two moving parts, you've got yourself a jet engine. Air is sucked into the engine and squeezed, by a compressor. Fuel is introduced to this compressed air and is ignited, or burned. Now the hot, expanding gases are given a hole in the rear of the engine from which to blow. Natural law says that for every action, there is an opposite and equal reaction. If you squirt hot gases out the back of the engine, then the engine, and everything bolted to it, will start moving forward, unless you've tied them down.

Take yourself a big tube and put a rotating drum inside it. Stick a lot of little propellor blades on the drum so that, when the drum turns, air is moved to the back of the tube. Now, make the drum fatter at the rear than it is in the front, and as you move the air back, it is squeezed, compressed. When you have gotten about all of the squeeze you can get, add a little fuel, kerosene actually, and light the mixture. Whoof, the mixture of fuel and air burns and expands. Since there is still air coming in the front of the engine, the hot gases can't get out that way, so they head for the big hole in the back of the engine, the tailpipe. On the way out, these gases have one critical thing left to do: they must pass over another set of little propellor blades that drive the turbine wheel. The turbine wheel is attached to a long shaft that goes back to the front of the engine and turns the drum, or compressor. The compressor drum, the shaft and the turbine wheel can be thought of as one piece, turning in large ball bearings.

But, I said two moving parts, didn't I? O.K., let's add another turbine wheel behind the first and force the hot exhaust over it also. Screw this wheel onto a smaller shaft and run it through the center of the other, hollow shaft and add another compressor "stage" to the front of the engine. There you have two moving parts, each carefully balanced, spinning happily along, making the stuff of flight — thrust.

Occasionally an engine will fail. The author once noted that one of his two engines was developing less thrust than the other and, after landing, had the mechanics check it out. The verdict? Almost one third of the little blades on both turbine wheels had sheared off. That poor, abused engine was still capable of giving me enough thrust to maintain flight, even if the other engine had failed completely.

Incidently, the incident described above is the only instance where I have encountered any kind of problem with these JT-8D engines in over 17 years and almost 11,000 flying hours, which include the blizzards of Boston and Toronto, and the suffocating heat of Miami and Tuscon. Your Oldsmobile should be so reliable.

NAVIGATION SYSTEMS

Frequently, a flight attendant will enter the cockpit and announce that a passenger wants to know "What is that town over there?" I would ask on which side of the airplane he was seated.

"He's on the left side."

I would glance out of the window and answer, "That's White Feather, North Carolina, down there."

Satisfied, she would return to the cabin with a personal position report for her passenger.

I did this for some years, always using the name "White Feather" along with whatever state that I suspected we were over.

Finally it caught up with me. Shortly after telling the flight attendant that we were over White Feather, North Carolina, she returned and repeated her passenger's opinion that I didn't know where I was.

"He said that last week, you told him he was over White

Feather, Texas, and a month ago it was White Feather, South Carolina. He demands to know where we are."

Since we happened to be passing near Greensboro, North Carolina, I dutifully copied the latitude and longitude numbers on a scrap of paper, and gave it to the worried young lady.

"Tell him we passed over this, two minutes and seventeen seconds ago...and take him a drink with my compliments for having such a memory."

The passenger, in fact, was right. I only happened by chance, to recognize the oil storage tanks near the airport of that beautiful southern city. But very few pilots, no matter how long they have been flying any given route, can tell you where they are by looking out the window, unless they are over a large, easily-identifed landmark. It has been many years since airliners were navigated by recognizing landmarks. It is all done by radios of various types. Here again, there is a lot of redundancy.

The primary means of navigation is a radio system known as the VOR (for Visual Omni Range). There are hundreds of these radio stations scattered over America and most of the world. Each airliner has at least two but usually three receivers that translate the radio's signals into useful work, such as telling you where you are.

Simply dial in the frequency of the desired station and select, on another dial, the course you want to follow to, or from, that station. A left/right needle on the instrument panel will tell you which way to steer the airplane to stay on that course. Remember, the word "course" refers to a line across the ground, and not the way that the airplane is pointed (heading). Automatically selected, when dialing in a VOR frequency, is a second signal called DME (Distance Measuring Equipment). This tells you in a simple digital readout how far you are from the selected station.

A much older system, and less precise, is the Automatic Direction Finder, very much the same as that carried by most ships at sea. Still used for long range overwater flights, this radio system is primarily used to locate the weak stations that comprise a part of the Instrument Landing Systems serving most airports. These receivers (usually two are installed) are quite capable of being used for navigation if all of the VOR receivers were to fail.

THE AUTOMATIC PILOT

Aircraft used for very long range flights such as over ocean trips to Europe or the Orient, carry two and sometimes three Inertial Navigation Systems, or INSs. These very precise "Gyro Platform" type units do not need to receive any radio signals from any source at all. Once you "initialize" the unit (tell it where it is), you simply tell it where you want to go, hook it up to the Automatic Pilot and away you go, on an exact course. While one INS tells the Autopilot where to steer, the other one keeps the first one honest by keeping a running double check on its navigation. The third one keeps an eye on the other two. Since all three are initialized and programmed independently, the odds of ever being off course are extremely remote, however... !

One INS is designated as the master and the others are "slaves." You can program the route that you want to follow into the master and send that program to the slaves with the push of a button. Any error in the master's programming will be sent, exactly, to the slaves and no discrepancy will ever show up. The airplane will obediently fly the commands of the master and the slaves will never know the difference. This is why all airlines insist that each INS be programed separately. People make mistakes, but the chances of entering the same mistake into three different systems are negligible. With the INS priced at something near $100,000 each, you can see that the airlines take their long range navigation seriously.

A newer and cheaper (if you want to call somewhere around 40 or 50 thousand dollars "cheap") system is the Omega Navigation System (ONS).

There are seven or eight very low frequency stations located around the world. The signals from these stations have the ability to bend around the earth's curved surface and are receivable anywhere on the planet.

The ONS receives these signals, decides which are the strongest three, and ignores the rest. Then through simple triangulation and a computer that works so hard it must glow in the dark, the ONS will do everything but make coffee. But, just like INS, the ONS system will fly the airplane while you drink the coffee.

If, through some terrible thing that you may have done to aggravate the gods of chance, all of this fails, all you need to do is pick up your trusty microphone and announce to Air Traffic Control people, on any one of three communications systems installed, that you have a problem and would appreciate a steering vector to anywhere with clear skies. If you have lost all navigation ability, it is because you have lost the electrical power that powers all of the radios and you will be anxious to land.

Redundancy is the pilot's way of carrying a full bag of marbles to the schoolyard and never playing them all.

Even so, most captains still carry around an old road atlas so they can point out Mt. St. Helens, the Painted Desert, Monument Valley, or a town called White Feather.

By now you may be approaching that stage called saturation: enough with the nuts and bolts.

I have said it before and I will say it again, I never expected you to close this book, wearing the mantle of expert on the jet airliner, with only the fragmented information I have covered so far. All I have tried to get across, with the examples I have used, is that the airplane, the crew, in fact, the whole air travel system, is designed so that things can fail and it won't matter. There is always a backup system to cover any failure. A lot of very bright, very concerned people have lain awake many sleepless nights dreaming up almost impossible ways for things to go wrong, then jumping out of bed to devise a procedure or system to cover that remote possibility. In the case of our 727, this refinement process has been going on for over 20 years.

PILOTS MAINTAIN A HEALTHY SKEPTICISM

Pilots, with all their training and experience, still maintain a healthy skepticism of all the rules, standards and procedures until they can prove, to their own satisfaction, that this is the safest way to do things. Not just safe enough, but the safest possible way that a thing can be done. Any pilot who does not have that feeling all the way down to his toenails has no business flying passengers, and very few do.

You have seen in this chapter that the airplane is a marvelous device with double, triple and often, quadruple levels of redundancy. This redundancy is even carried over to the pilots themselves. Either the captain or the copilot are qualified and capable of flying the airplane and, in most cases, the third man, the flight engineer, is also a pilot. Just as the machinery is designed so that no failure will have a serious effect, so it is with the crew. If a mistake is made by one pilot, the other will catch the error and correct it.

Now we have a fine airplane and a good crew, so we can just jump in and go blasting off. Not so fast. There are some 15,000 scheduled airline flights each day. That means a lot of airplanes whiz around the skies. Since no one has the desire to "swap paint" with anyone else, there has to be some sort of structure, some order to all of this mass of machinery.

We need to take a look at how all of these aircraft are kept separated. After all, we are still dealing with one of those physical laws: the one that states that no two bodies can occupy the same space at the same time.

CHAPTER 5

AIR TRAFFIC CONTROL

Air Traffic Control is a many layered system. Many controllers labor over radar scopes, keeping track of enroute flights in the medium and high altitude structures. Other controllers operate the airspace near airports and still others operate the control towers. These are the front line controllers but there are still more behind-the-lines people who handle clearances, operate the maze of computers and maintain the whole, gigantic business.

An air traffic controller is employed by the Federal Aviation Administration. This massive government agency, through its many departments, is responsible for the safe operation of the nation's airways, highways in the sky. They hire and train the controllers. Let us take a brief glimpse at the air traffic controller.

THE TRAINING PROGRAM

Some years ago, virtually all controllers were hired directly from the military. These young men all had at least two years of controlling experience, usually more. It was good experience. Keeping track of a bunch of supersonic fighters, often under emergency conditions, will keep one alert. Now, however, there is a lack of these military people and the agency has been forced to lower its hiring requirements.

After extensive testing, the new trainee would attend the FAA's training facility in Oklahoma City. There he or she will enter a nine week training course that includes radar and computer training. Then they go "to a facility."

Just as in the cockpit, here is where the real training begins: experience with real traffic in a real environment. The new controller will observe for quite a while, then he will sit down at the radar scope. When he keys his microphone, he is talking to a real pilot with real concerns.

Always, though, there is an experienced supervisor controller watching over the new fellow's shoulder and, even more importantly, listening to every word that is said. He is listening to how it is said, the strain in the controller's voice. This supervisor has, in his hand, an "overriding" microphone. If the trainee says anything that the supervisor does not like or if he gives a poorly judged instruction, the supervisor need only press a button on his mike and he is instantly in control of the situation. He has blocked the other controller's ability to transmit: he has taken over. It will be quite a while before the controller will actually control air traffic without that supervisor standing behind him, following his every move and word.

Controllers have been discribed as egotistical and, sometimes, overbearing. I prefer to think of them as confident. I do not want a person controlling my flight who is unsure of himself. I do not want anything of a tentative nature in his instructions.

The best way to understand how complex the system really is would be to follow just the radio contacts an airliner must make during a flight. Let's go back to our flight from LaGuardia to Atlanta, two high density airports. This time you are sitting in the cockpit with a pair of headphones.

CLEARANCE BEFORE A FLIGHT TAKES OFF

First the copilot will dial in a frequency and listen to ATIS (Automatic Terminal Information Service). This is a tape recorded message that gives information on current weather, runways in use and any critical safety information that might affect a pilot's decision on his runway of choice. Often the airport may be using a runway based on noise considerations, which pilots are usually happy to accept. Pilots want to be good neighbors to the surrounding communities. On rare occasions the airplane may be too heavy or the wind direction will not permit takeoff on the prefered "noise abatement" runway and the pilot will make that request later.

The copilot will then change to another frequency, and call "Clearance Delivery." Here a controller will read the flight's ATC clearance, which the copilot will copy, in his unique shorthand, and read back verbatim.

Let's spend a moment with the Air Traffic Control clearance that each flight must have before it takes off.

A route and altitude is filed in the airline's computer. The dispatcher for the line will inspect the weather along the route and, if satisfied, direct the computer to send the flight plan directly to the ATC facility. This flight plan is placed in the ATC computer and then sent to the "Clearance Delivery" position at the airport of departure.

An hour before departure, the flight crew will begin going over the dispatch papers for the flight. The captain will note the route and do his own weather inspection. If he feels good about the flight, he will determine the fuel he wants for the trip, sign a dispatch release and head for the airplane. If he detects a weather pattern that might give him trouble, he will call the dispatcher and talk things over. They may jointly decide on a change of route, and the dispatcher enters the revised route in the airline's computer which will then send it to the air traffic control center. It takes these two people, the captain and the dispatcher, to agree that a flight can be safely flown.

When the copilot calls for the clearance, he is given the following message:

"Antares 242, you are cleared as filed via the Ringos One departure, Westminster transition. Climb to 5000 feet and expect flight level three five zero ten minutes after departure. Squawk 3735, Departure control is on 120.4."

The air traffic control computer has checked the requested route and notified a controller to clear the flight "as filed."

The "Ringos One" departure is a published departure route for aircraft leaving La Guardia southwest bound. After a series of turns that may be designed to hold the noise down, the flight would turn toward a radio fix located at Solberg, N.J., then turn along a crooked path to Westminster, Pennsylvania. The copilot was told to maintain 5000 feet and to expect FL350, 10 minutes after departure. The flight can climb only to 5000 feet initially, but, in the event of a radio failure shortly after takeoff, he could climb to 35,000 feet after 10 minutes. This would give ATC time to clear everything out of his way. If he were forced to remain at 5000 feet, he would not be able to travel very far to find a good airport. Jet engines burn a tremendous amount of precious fuel at the low altitudes. (Remember, the weather was pretty snowy at LaGuardia, and he could not return without radios.) By climbing to his cruise altitude, he could then continue all the way to his destination or, knowing the weather in Atlanta, find a place that he could land in the clear.

The copilot was told to call LaGuardia departure control on frequency 120.4, after becoming airborne, and was told to set his transponder to a distinctive code that would identify his flight to ATC controllers.

After the engines are started, the copilot (hard working young fellow, isn't he) will call "ground control" for taxi clearance. "Ground control" is a controller, up in the control tower, whose responsibility it is to keep traffic moving around the airport taxiways, to prevent airplanes from snarling into an immovable mass. Many airports have two ground controllers, each working different sides of the airport.

Approaching the active runway, the copilot will switch to the "tower." Another controller, in the control tower, is controlling flights taking off and landing. He has access to a short range radar, some binoculars, a well used radio microphone and a very, very steady nerve. He clears Antares 242 for takeoff.

CLEARANCE AFTER DEPARTURE

Immediately after takeoff, the tower will ask the flight to "contact departure control." Another shift of frequencies and the copilot is now talking to another controller in a darkened room, well below the tower. From now until he contacts Atlanta tower, all of the controllers will be in one dimly lit "radar room" or another, halfway across the country. These people don't even have a window in the room, yet they can "see" for hundreds of miles.

After some steering orders, the departure controller will change the flight to "New York Southwest Departure." On another frequency, another controller whose radar scans the 40 odd miles southwest of the New York area's four major airports. This controller's main responsibility is to integrate all departing flights along their outbound airways, stepping the flights up in altitude, while keeping the inbound airways clear for arriving flights, who are talking on another frequency to any of three "approach controls."

"Southwest departure, Antares 242, level at five thousand."

"Roger, Antares 242, climb to 16 thousand and you are

cleared direct to Solberg, over."

"Antares 242 is leaving five for one six thousand and going to Solberg."

After the rapid fire communications with the close in, New York City area controllers, it is a relief to hear, "Antares 242, contact New York Center on 124.6. Good day, sir."

"Roger, '24.6. Antares 242, good day." The copilot contacts New York Air Route Traffic Control Center.

"New York, Antares 242, level at 16 thousand."

When switching frequencies the copilot alternates between two radios. If he were to be confused on a frequency, he would always have the previous frequency already set up in the other radio. He would also be certain that both radios were operating normally. Redundancy at work.

"Good evening, Antares 242, climb to and maintain flight level 230."

The flight is now in contact with one small segment of the enroute structure of New York Center. This controller will be controlling a small piece of airspace along certain airways, and at altitudes below 24,000 feet.

A word on altitude. From the ground up to 18,000 feet, a controller will speak in terms of "thousands of feet." To say one–two thousand is to say twelve thousand. At 18,000 feet and above, everything is said to be a "flight level." This flight level is given in the first three digits. To clear an airplane to climb to twenty-five thousand feet is said in a clearance, "Climb and maintain flight level two five zero." The last two digits of the altitude, 25,000, are left off.

Just before reaching flight level 230 (FL), New York Center calls:

"Antares 242, call Washington Center, 133.6. Have a nice flight."

The copilot calls Washington Center and the controller there gives clearance to climb to FL350. As you climb through FL 280, Washington center calls back. "Antares 242, now maintain flight level 290, over."

"Roger, Antares 242 will maintain 290 . . . about to level."

"Antares 242, check 11 o'clock. Northbound traffic at 310."

"Roger, we have contact." The crew watches as the twinkling anti-collision lights of the northbound flight sweep by, close enough to see the lights of the cabin glowing

in a line of little squares. The captain reaches up and briefly flashes his landing light at the passing airplane. A silent,
"Good evening, sir. Have a nice flight." Just as the other
airplane flashes by, an answering stab of brilliance, ". . . and
to you, as well." Then he is gone.

"Antares 242, you are clear of traffic, climb to flight
level 350, and you are cleared direct to Gordonsville." Even
though the actual airway makes several slight turns before
reaching the navigational radio called Gordonsville, the
controller has checked his radar and found no conflicting
traffic between the flight and Gordonsville. He has cleared
you to fly direct: a little short cut.

The pilot acknowledges and resumes his climb.

AVERTING A POTENTIAL CONFLICT

The controller has been monitoring your progress and so has
a sophisticated computer, which has also been tracking the
traffic and has caused the airplane to stop its climb. The
computer alerted the controller of a potential conflict, two
airplanes about to occupy the same "envelope" of airspace,
and he stopped the climb before an actual conflict could
occur. At this time the airplane is actually in the center of
a big, invisible "box" with 1000 feet above, 1000 feet below
and 10 miles surrounding it in all directions. No other
flight's "box" can touch any edge of Antares 242's box.

These controllers are watching a radar display that in-
corporates lines that depict the boundaries of his airspace,
any airways within his sector, weather returns, and every
airplane within his area of responsibility.

Your flight appears to him as a little group of letters and
numbers. This little "box" travels along as you cross his
scope, along with any other airplanes in his sector. Veteran
controllers refer to this box as a "Shrimp Boat," recalling
the earlier days when flights were tracked with a small boat
shaped marker with a tiny flag that displayed the flight's
information.

At the upper altitudes, where you are flying, all airplanes are separated by 2,000 feet. If any two airplanes
were to be anywhere near each other and less than a difference of 2,000 feet should exist, the computer will alert
the controller who can provide evasive maneuvers if necessary. If any aircraft should stray more than 250 feet from
his assigned altitude, the computer will flash an "altitude

alert" to the controller, and at the same time, a yellow light will begin flashing in the cockpit along with an aural "Beep, Beep, Beep." The computer will automatically file a deviation report to the FAA enforcement offices and someone will be writing letters. Pilots do not enjoy writing letters.

THE APPROACH AND LANDING

Over the next hour your aircraft will switch frequencies about eight more times as it flies from one control center sector to the next. You will contact Atlanta Air Traffic Control Center while still over Tennessee. At about 100 miles from Atlanta, the flight will be cleared to begin its descent and the copilot will tune the standby radio to the Atlanta ATIS frequency to get the field's landing information.

"This is Atlanta arrival information Romeo. All aircraft shall read back all runway holding instructions, including aircraft identification. Atlanta weather at zero one fifteen Greenwich, variable two hundred overcast, one half mile visibility, light rain and fog. Temperature four nine, dewpoint four seven, wind two three zero at three knots. Altimeter two nine eight two. Landing runways two seven left and two six right. Notice to airmen, runway two six left is closed. Advise Atlanta approach control on initial contact that you have information Romeo."

"Atlanta Approach, this is Antares 242, with Romeo, out of 17 thousand for 16 thousand." By telling the approach controller that he has "Romeo," he has assured the controller that he has the latest information. If anything has changed at the airport, the ATIS will begin broadcasting information "Sierra." The controller will then tell the flight to listen to this latest information.

"Roger, Antares 242, continue your descent to 11 thousand and slow to 210 knots. You will be landing runway 27 left, frequency 108.5." To make absolutely certain that the crew knows the runway on which it is to land, the controller has not only named the runway but the frequency of the navigational radio that will lead the airplane to the runway. An airplane with the wrong radio frequency tuned in could really stir up a busy airport traffic pattern.

"Antares 242 is cleared to 11 thousand and we are slowing to 210...27 left for us."

You are now entering the infamous "combat zone." To approach and land at Atlanta, Georgia requires that an airman be very professional and pay close attention. The approach controller working your flight and 20 others doesn't have time to repeat himself in the event that you missed a radio transmission. To listen to the machine gun chatter of an approach controller is to hear a man who is almost in another dimension. His mind is racing along at a pace that very few other men could comprehend: vectoring airplanes, closing up distances, forming orderly lines— making some sort of order out of apparent chaos. After only a few minutes with this gentleman, your flight is switched over to the "final approach controller" who will further refine the line of blips on his radar scope and give vectors onto the final approach course. The working relationship between these two controllers is a joy to contemplate. The two are literally thinking as one. You wish that you could have complimented the first controller on his work, but with the same transmission that changed you over to the final controller, he was already talking to three other flights, who were also paying attention. There simply is no time for a "nice job."

"Final" slows you to 180 knots and gives you a new course to fly:

"Antares 242, turn right heading 250, intercept the localizer, maintain 180 to the marker. You are cleared for the approach to 27L. Contact the tower on 119.1 at the marker."

With this rattle of words, the final approach controller has told you to fly a compass heading of 250 degrees until receiving the radio navigational signal that will guide you to the runway. You must fly a speed of 180 knots until you pass over a small radio transmitter that will sound a tone in your headset and flash a blue light on the panel. This signal and light (both of them) are called the outer marker. Then you can slow to your final approach speed. "Cleared for the approach" means that when the radio signal that provides vertical guidance is received, you may start your descent to the runway. He has also told you to contact the control tower when you pass over the outer marker.

"Antares 242, roger. We are cleared for the approach." Off to your right you see another airplane lined up on the other runway. You are still out in clear air with the fog below you.

Now you start to descend. "Gear down, final checklist."

As the fog enshrouds the world outside, the pulsating tone is heard, and the blue light begins to flash on the instrument panel. The captain's instruments should indicate that he is on the glideslope and over the outer marker at the same time. Another little bit of redundancy.

"Atlanta Tower, Antares 242, by the marker, 27L."

"Antares 242, you are number two for the runway. 27L RVR is 2400 feet...break...Delta 1049, right turn at the high speed, hold short of 27R and stay with me. Your traffic is rolling...let me know when you see him pass you." You have been informed that there is one airplane in front of you and the visibility in feet (2400). Then, with no time to release his mike button, the tower controller has switched his attentions to Delta flight 1049 by saying "break." He has told Delta to turn off the runway on an angled taxiway and to stop before crossing the parallel runway. Since the tower controller is unable to see the runway, he has told Delta to inform him when the airplane on its takeoff roll, on that parallel runway, passes him.

"Antares 242, are we cleared to land?" Before landing, the crew must hear and acknowledge a clearance to land. Without those words, they would have to pull up.

"Antares 242, you are cleared to land, runway 27L, RVR holding at 2400 feet. Wind is calm."

"This is Delta 1049. We just had some lights go by us."

"Roger, Delta 1049, cross 27R, ground point eight on the other side. Good night gentlemen." The Delta flight has been cleared to cross runway 27R and to call the ground controller on 121.8 mHz. He has also had time to say good night.

Up in the tower, the lights are dimmed to their lowest level and six people are talking softly but swiftly into boom type microphones. They are watching several radar displays, not even bothering to look out of the gray, misted windows. The most they could expect to see would be a fast moving glow of landing lights as they appeared near the end of the runway, if they could see the end of the runway. Occasionally, the fog will lift enough for the tower operators to see the glow of the runway lights and a brighter ball of light as an airplane arrives or departs. But, for the most part, they remain isolated up in the mist. They, and the controllers who will relieve them, will spend the entire shift without seeing an airplane.

"Antares 242, right turn at the high speed turnoff, hold short of 27R and stay with me...acknowledge." Acknowledge! He wants to be damned sure that you heard him say to stop short of the other runway, only a quarter mile away. There is another 727 blasting down that runway. He wants you to say so. Remember the ATIS message. "All aircraft shall read back all runway holding instructions, including aircraft identification." No airman or controller will ever forget the foggy day at the Tenerife airport when a KLM 747 slammed into a Pan American 747. One captain THOUGHT that the runway was clear. It wasn't. The controllers are very, very careful at Atlanta. This is not a business where one can THINK he is right. He must KNOW he is right.

"Antares 242, Roger, we will hold short of the right side."

Atlanta's Hartsfield Airport has four parallel runways, running east and west. Two of these runways are on the north side of the airport and two are on the south side. Of these two south runways, 27Right is used for takeoffs and 27Left is for landings. Over on the north side of the airport, runway 26Left is used for takeoff and 26Right is for landing traffic. Runways are named for the magnetic heading a compass will display when lined up on the runway. Since all four of Atlanta's runways are aligned alike, it avoids confusion to name one set of runways 27 (L and R) and the other set, 26 (L and R) even though the compass headings are the same. (Pittsburgh, with three parallel runways, can call its runways, 28Left, 28Center and 28Right.)

"Antares 242, now cross 27R and contact ground control on 121.8."

"Antares 242 is cleared to cross the right. Good night, sir."

"Good night...Eastern 182, cleared to land on 27L, RVR is 1800 feet variable 2200 feet." (The visibility is lowering. You may have arrived in Atlanta just in time.)

"Atlanta Ground, Antares 242 is clear of the 27R."

TAXIING FROM THE RUNWAY

"Welcome to the sunny south, Antares 242, taxi to the ramp via the inner taxiway. What is your ramp number?"

"Ramp 4, if we can find it in all this sunshine."

"Just follow the yellow brick road, and give way to an

outbound Eastern L-1011 coming out of Ramp 3." That yellow brick road is actually a taxi-way lined with blue lights, and it often has a line of green lights running down its center line. Easier to follow in heavy fog. You are down, safe. No matter how many times you fly a close approach, there is always a tremendous release of emotion when it is over. "Sunny South" and "Yellow brick road" are not official, government approved things to say over an airplane radio. Nonetheless, they are said and they will continue to be said. The ground controller is also happy.

"Roger, we'll give way to Eastern."

You think that you are glad that it is a huge L-1011 that you are trying to see; this stuff is thick. You see the massive gray shape of the heavy Lockheed moving, the fog swirling in the beam of its nose wheel taxi light, and you proceed to the next ramp and change frequencies one last time. Each of the five ramps that separate the "airside" terminals has its own little ground control, operated by the airline that occupies most of the gates.

"Ramp 4, Antares 242 is coming in on the south side."

"Come in on the right side of the ramp, Antares. There is a heavy Airbus being pushed off the gate to your left. You are cleared to the gate."

There is gate D 21 and as the airplane begins to turn into the gate, the pilot switches off the taxi lights, so they do not blind the signalman who will direct your nose wheel to a painted spot that will align the airplane's door with the jetway.

The second officer has the last word on our flight. He calls on the company frequency, "242 On at :42, In at :47, 13,000 pounds of fuel on board, outbound fuel, 33,000." The flight touched down at 42 minutes past the hour and parked at 47 minutes past. They had 13,000 pounds of fuel remaining in the ship's tanks. The captain wanted 33,000 pounds of fuel pumped onboard for the flight back to New York.

The company agent repeats the times that you landed and parked and the fuel remaining on board, then adds, "You may want to recheck the outbound fuel, sir. LaGuardia is getting pretty crummy."

That little snowstorm that you left is getting serious now.

Even as the passengers file off of the 727, over in the Air Traffic Control Center the machinery is already in motion for Antares 247, a Boeing 727, from Atlanta to New York via the LaGuardia terminal. A computer printer rattles off the clearance.

"Antares 247 is not going to like this," says one ATC specialist to another, as he tears off a notice of lengthy delays into LaGuardia. "New York is not a very nice place to be headed tonight."

"Hell, Atlanta is not all that pleasant tonight," his co-worker observes, then adds, "We are likely to go down within the hour and there will be airplanes scattered all over the southeast U.S. of A."

"Yeah, tomorrow the morning shift should be a lot of fun."

The printer buzzes off seven more clearances and a phone rings.

"We've got a gate hold on all New York departures... 30 minutes for now."

Not too long ago, the air traffic control people would allow anyone to takeoff on schedule, even if the destination weather was known to be bad. Within a short time, the sky over that destination would be full of airplanes, milling around in holding patterns, burning precious fuel and, often, having to divert to some alternate airport. Now, departures are held at the gate, engines silent, until the system can accept them with a minimum of delay at their destination.

The snow removal crews at LaGuardia have fired up their heavy equipment and have begun to move toward the snow covered runways. For about an hour, the airport must be closed to air traffic and the runways swept. There will be delays, but it is better to have airplanes sitting at their gates in Chicago, Miami and Atlanta than to have them converging on the New York area only to be told to fly a holding pattern until their fuel starts running low — much better. Even the most impatient passenger would agree to this if he had a set of fuel quantity gauges to watch and another set of fuel flow gauges that showed a fuel burn of 8000 pounds of fuel per hour.

We need to take a look at how weather affects flight operations since no other factor has as much of an impact on your journey.

CHAPTER 6

WEATHER

The railroads used to make an issue of the fact that they ran on schedule. Period. This became a very serious thing to them and to those who rode the rails. Visions shimmer into mind of the old station master, standing at trackside, dwarfed only by the steaming, chuffing locomotive, with his railroad-issue pocket watch in hand. As the sweep second hand of the watch passed over the appointed time, the station master nodded at the engineer, and the train began to move. It mattered not if the station master's own mother were to be running down the platform, trying to catch the train. When departure time arrived the wheels began to turn.

A train is basically a two-dimensional creature. Its two tracks pretty well define its course while its weight and lack of meaningful aerodynamics keep it pretty close to the ground. About the only control one had was how fast or slow the beast was to travel. It also took a whopping great storm to affect its movements; therefore, the train could be generally be relied upon to maintain its schedule.

However, when you consider that any airplane flight that you take is going to be affected, in one way or another, by the weather, it is no small miracle that flights are not scheduled to arrive and depart on a particular day, rather than by listing an hour and minute. Perhaps the schedule should read:

"Antares flight 242 will leave LaGuardia, around 5:30 PM or so, depending on the weather."

Let me put something in perspective here. If you fly very often, the chances are that your flight will be delayed leaving the gate. In almost every case, the delay will have been caused by weather. The weather may be fine where you are, with sunny skies and soft breezes, but the airplane came to you from Boston, where there are fierce winds and snow, or from Kansas City where thunderstorms rumble near the airport. Somewhere back up the line, somewhere at some airport, flights are not operating as scheduled. These delays accumulate, and your evening departure from LaGuardia may very well be late. You might keep this in mind: early morning flights usually leave closer to schedule than do evening departures. It is not the fault of the airline. They can't possibly predict where the weather is going to be lousy when they make up the schedule.

THUNDERSTORMS

You can't blame the pilots who refuse to fly through thunderstorms just to keep the airplane on time. The air traffic control system cannot flow traffic smoothly through "Thunderstorm Alley," because the alley won't be in the same place within an hour.

When Mother Nature reaches down into her bag of tricks, mere mortal man must constantly revise and even re-invent the airline system with every passing hour.

Thunderstorms are old Mom's way of throwing a temper tantrum. There is no force on the planet Earth that can match the sheer, awesome power of the basic afternoon thunderstorm along the gulf coast of Florida or Texas. In these areas, conditions are perfect for the creation of air mass thunderstorms. Towering to heights of over 50,000 feet, these monsters can reduce runway visibilities to less than one-half mile in driving rain, kick up surface winds of 50 knots and close an airport. No one is going to knowingly fly an approach or departure in the midst of one of these giants. The happiest thing that can be said about an air mass thunderstorm is that it won't be there long. Usually, it will move off within 15 to 30 minutes.

If the air mass thunderstorm (usually scattered about and easily flown around) holds the deepest respect in the hearts of pilots, it is the frontal squall lines of thunderstorms that can turn those hearts to solid ice. A wedge of cold, Canadian air two thousand miles wide will push its way south. Like an immense snow plow, the front edge of this mass scoops up warm, moist air and sends it aloft, creating rain clouds, then thunderstorms. Lines of thunderstorms, hundreds of miles long, march along, shoulder to shoulder like monstrous centurions, their shields flashing almost continuously with lightning bolts. Often the violent surface winds of one storm will interact with those of its nearest neighbor and tornados will form, slashing through anything in their paths.

Sometimes there is a hole in the line (Ernest Gann describes these holes in his *Fate Is the Hunter* as "...a hole, small, but of exquisite design." I wish I had said that). Often there are no holes, and the prudent pilot must then fly many miles off of his planned course to find either a hole or the end of the line.

Somewhere in the history of each pilot's logbook rests the notation regarding the night when he tried for a hole that lured him in, toyed with him for a few brief moments, then slammed shut. This is called a "Sucker Hole." Having learned their lessons, very few pilots go for the "Sucker Hole" a second time.

WINDSHEAR

A deadly byproduct of a thunderstorm is windshear. Actually, this phenomenon has been around for a long time, but only gained national prominence when it was blamed for the crash of Eastern flight 66 at Kennedy Airport. An age-old enemy was simply given a name. Ten years later a Pan American 727 slammed into the surburbs of New Orleans and, again, windshear was cited as the probable cause of the accident. Most recently, in August of 1985, a Delta L-1011 crashed in driving rain at the Dallas/Ft. Worth airport. Once more, windshear has been pinned down as the cause.

As a result of these accidents, training has intensified at the airlines. Models of the known weather conditions are programmed into the simulator and pilots are required to face those conditions and fly through them. New techniques have been designed for coping with windshear and, after a few of the demonstrations, many pilots are vowing not to enter any weather that has the potential for windshear.

Let's take a look at the genesis of a windshear incident. A thunderstorm forms when warm, moist air is lifted aloft. As this air rises, it cools and begins to form tiny water droplets. As more moist air is carried aloft, these small droplets join hands and form larger drops. The drops become large enough and heavy enough that they begin to fall back to earth. For a while, these falling drops of rain simply evaporate during their descent and rejoin still other warm air as it is rising. A vertical pattern of air movement develops, rather like having several elevators all operating at once, some up and some down.

The descending air and water in the center of the cloud forms the core or down elevator, while air is being carried aloft around the outer perimeter. What has been, until now, a simple cumulus cloud appears to be boiling and climbing at a very rapid rate. Inside the developing cell, as these systems are called, water drops have been growing in size and falling at a faster pace, dragging the surrounding air with them. Falling at almost the same rate as the air around it, the water has no chance to evaporate and comes out the bottom of the cloud. Rain is now reaching the earth, but the cycle continues. The friction of these opposing masses of air, some rising and some falling, creates electrical charges which, when reaching a full potential, discharge in the form of lightning and thunder.

Finally, the poor old storm has had enough. Masses of water have accumulated near the top and start to descend very rapidly. Down through the core a heavy column of water plummets, dragging even more air along with it. At the bottom of the cloud it doesn't even slow down but continues on to earth where it is finally stopped. The huge collection of descending air must now go somewhere so it splays out in all directions, causing wind velocities of up to 80 knots in some extreme cases.

The actual appearance of this mass of water and descending air is called a microburst. The discharge of all that energy can be over within only a few seconds' time, and that is the really insidious thing about the microburst and its attendant sudden blast of wind. By the time you see it, even on Doppler radar, and attempt to warn a flight of its presence, it is gone.

Current "Windshear Alert" installations at some airports around the country are almost worse than useless. By the time an overworked controller recognizes the alert and transmits the information in a long, cumbersome and confusing radio transmission, and the pilot of an approaching airliner hears and deciphers this string of words, the microburst and windshear have come and gone. Human speech simply takes too long.

Suffice it to say that a growing number of pilots are

increasingly reluctant to enter any weather, especially during the landing or takeoff phase of flight, during which there is even the potential for a microburst, and that means when there is thunderstorm activity near the airport.

Remember that any storm that does have this potential is moving right along on its own. It will not be in the vicinity for long: usually not more than fifteen or twenty minutes. So delays will be minimal.

LIGHTNING

It is time for a myth to be put to rest: that of lightning and its effect on airplanes.

Anchorman Dan Handsome, his face stern, describes the site of an airplane accident and adds, to what little he has already said, the comment, "...and it has been reported that lightning was observed in the area."

The clear implication is that lightning had a hand in bringing the airplane down. Bullfeathers! Lightning strikes many airplanes every day. The very loud report may have a dramatic effect on unsuspecting passengers, but apart from that, it is harmless. No one is electrocuted or even singed. A heavy strike may pop a few circuit breakers in the airplane's electrical system, but these are reset and all is well.

As an airplane flies through rain or dry snow, the friction of the moisture on the skin of the ship begins to build a static charge, just as you do when you walk across a carpeted hallway to the door of, say, a hotel room. You reach out with your key and ZAP! You may even see a tiny spark leap between the key and the grounded doorknob.

In the airplane, you will rarely see static electricity being built up while you are seated in the cabin but, up in the cockpit, the effect is quite noticeable. First, sparks begin to play about on the windshield wiper. Then the edges of the windshield frame begin to glow with blue fire. Soon the entire windshield will be alive with tiny blue discharges, and sparkling blue "fingers" of the icy fire begin to reach out beyond the nose of the aircraft, searching for a place to release all of this stored energy. The entire windshield looks not unlike your TV screen when you tune to a channel that is not transmitting a picture, except the electronic excitement is blue and only a few inches from your eyes.

The airplane itself has become highly charged with static

electricity. As the ship moves further through the clouds, it may approach another cloud possessing an opposite charge. If the charge is sufficient in either the airplane or the cloud...BANG! You have not merely been hit by lightning but have been an actual part of the discharge itself.

While this writer has never seen it, there are tales of "ball lightning" that guarantee a thrilling moment. When flying through these same clouds that can build a static charge, a "ball" of electrical energy (described as about the size of a basketball) will form inside the airplane and literally roll down the aisle. Imagine yourself watching such a glowing, sparkling mass of—something, approaching your seat. You have every right in the world to be at least mildly interested. However, knowing that the phenomenon is harmless (it is), you can lean over to your horrified seatmate and exclaim, "Not to worry, it's just ball lightning. It will go away." (It will.) Then try to yawn in boredom and you will be forever established in that person's mind as the original "Joe Cool."

Ball lightning does not seem to be as frequent with the jet airplanes as it was in the older propeller aircraft, leading one to believe that the whirling propellers created more static electricity than the jets. If this is so, good riddance!

Leaving aside your startled nerve endings, the only effect that lightning will have in the airplane is the slight smell of ozone, quickly dispelled by the air conditioning system. The bolt will enter, usually around the nose of the bird, and exit near the trailing edge of a wing or the tail surfaces. The only evidence of its passage are tiny burn marks, usually no more than a few thousandths of an inch in diameter. I have been hit several times and the worst damage has been a dime-sized blister on the plastic radome that forms the nose of the aircraft.

When possible, the crew will slow the machine, reducing the friction and allowing the "static wicks," little prongs located on the trailing edges of all control surfaces, to dissipate the static.

Incidently, if you are beginning to draw a parallel between what I have described and the Ancient Mariner's "St. Elmo's Fire," you are exactly correct.

You must go back to the 1950s to find the only case of a jet being brought down by lightning. Shortly after its introduction to airline service, a Boeing 707 was struck directly in a fuel vent pipe. The spark ignited fuel vapors in the pipe, which traveled back up the pipe into the almost empty fuel tank and the tank exploded. Within weeks, all 707 fuel vents were modified with lightning arrester devices that precluded a repeat of this kind of accident. As I have said, lightning strikes airplanes daily, with no effect. This writer has been hit several times.

FOG

Fog is another of Mother Nature's little surprises, lowering visibilities to very low values. The saving grace of fog flying is that one of the conditions necessary to produce fog is calm winds. You can fly a very precise instrument approach when you are not being banged around by turbulence.

It was on just such a gray, fog-bound day that one of the flight attendants, a new young woman on the line, came forward into the cockpit after we had reached the gate.

"How in the world do you fellows find your way through all of this fog?" she asked.

My copilot turned wearily and said, "Cap'n does it all the time. He's had the operation."

"What operation?" she asked, as her lips closed daintily on the hook he had offered.

"THE operation...all of our captains have it done."

She inspected me for signs of a lobotomy, and again bit, "I don't understand...what operation?"

"When one of our pilots makes captain, they remove his cornea and transplant those of a duck. As everybody knows, ducks can see through the clouds."

She looked intently at my eyes and, I swear, she said, "They don't really do that, do they?"

What is a fellow to do? I looked back at her and gave her my best "QUACK."

When the merriment had subsided, she again asked "Really, how do you fly through all this fog?"

I answered with all of the sincerity I could muster, "Actually, Maryann, it has nothing to do with duck's eye transplants. It's really nothing more than simple magic." She smiled and wandered back into the cabin. I wasn't trying to be cruel but it would have taken quite a while to explain the intricate nature of instrument flight.

This brings us to a shortcoming of landing in heavy fog. It is common practice to fly approaches and land with cloud bases at 100 feet and the visibility around one quarter of a mile — something on the order of 1000 feet of visibility. The precision approach instruments make it almost easy to land a heavy airplane at 150 miles per hour. But then you face the task of groping your way through the mist to the terminal building: there are no radio aids or instruments along your murky way. Ground controllers at major airports can help some with expanded "taxi radar" showing all of the taxiways, runways and the airplanes thereon. This radar is not designed to actually guide airplanes.

I once strained to find my way from the runway to the Jacksonville, Florida, airport terminal. The mist was all but impenetrable. An occasional light would appear, but offered little in the way of real guidance. I moved slowly (what would my boss say if I called him from Jacksonville and told him I had just parked one of his DC-9s in the mud). Finally, seeing a dim glow in the fog that I took to be the terminal ramp, and the faint outline of a taxiway to take me there, I turned in.

"Cap'n, sir," my trusty copilot intoned, "There's something wrong here."

"I do believe you are right, youngster," I said as I also spotted the dark outline of half a dozen Cessnas and Pipers. We had turned onto the wrong taxiway, and inched our way onto the the private aircraft parking area. Fortunately, I was able to turn around and finally find my way to the proper parking ramp with the help of a startled lineman.

I mumbled something to my passengers about birds not even being so foolish as to walk around in such muck, parked my airplane and went to the hotel. I hoped I would not see any of those passengers in the lobby. I did. I decided not to offer the story about the operation.

ICE AND FREEZING RAIN

During the winter months, freezing drizzle often accompanies the fog. Jet airliners have little trouble handling icing conditions; heated wings and windshields remain clear of the frosty stuff. Airports do not enjoy all of this protection, however, and light rain, or drizzle, can form an icy sheath on the runways and taxiways in a few minutes. To land an airplane going like blue blazes and find yourself on the equivalent of a large skating rink will leave you with moments to remember. I often think of the pilots who frequent the Pittsburgh airport during the coming of the snows. The runways there are straightforward enough, but the taxiways are over hill and dale with great, deep ravines on either side. I do not know if anyone has ever slid off the edge of the world in Pittsburgh, but I try to fly mostly Florida trips during the icing season. Airport ice control crews are quick to scatter sand on these taxiways.

Compared to the glare ice that comes along with freezing drizzle, snow is almost a joy to work with, until the blizzards bring gusty crosswinds. With the vertical tail surface catching the winds like a big weathervane and the tires reluctant to grip an ice-covered surface, moving around an airport in high winds can also leave one with memories.

Take the night we approached the Kennedy Airport with winds reported at 52 knots, but right down the runway. The airport had been gripped in one of the worst, most prolonged cold snaps in New York's history and the surface of the airport was like oiled glass. Landing and stopping was no problem, but then came the task of swinging the tail around across that 52-knot wind and inching our way to the terminal. The little DC-9, built low to the ground, was able to negotiate the trip with only a few sideways excursions. But, as we moved along, we passed many larger airplanes — 747s, DC-10s and the like — whose massive size worked against them. They caught the wind and simply slid off the taxiway into the frozen mud. To a half a million pound airplane, mud is mud, frozen or not. It was days before they got the mess cleaned up, but first they had to get the passengers off the airplanes in the howling, frigid wind, and that took half of the buses in New York City.

CLEAR AIR TURBULENCE

Last in our weather summary is a brief explanation of CAT ...Clear Air Turbulence. Say that you are cruising along at high altitude, and the airplane starts to shake around a bit, not bad, nothing as bad as a cab ride through the potholes of New York or Washington, D.C., just annoying. Soon the chop becomes more pronounced and your full wine glass threatens to slosh its contents out. The seat belt sign comes on and the captain asks you to return to your seat and fasten your seatbelt. A few more minutes pass and the turbulence continues to build in intensity, yet you can see out the window that there is not a cloud in sight. The skies are as clear as crystal. You feel the airplane start to descend and things smooth out.

Chances are that you were cruising near the jet stream, an invisible river of fast moving air that flows across the nation. Normally over Canada and the northern states during summer, the jet stream shifts to the south when winter arrives and drops down to lower altitudes.

If your airplane approaches a jet stream, you will begin to get light turbulence because the air surrounding the river is being stirred by eddies, just as eddies form along the banks of an earthbound stream. If there were a way to get in the center of the stream, the chop would disappear, and if you were traveling east, you could get quite a boost from the tailwinds. The problem is that you never know whether you are in the center or just angling across it.

If you happened to come upon a jet stream which was traveling in the same direction as your airplane, suddenly the speed of the airplane would drop and, infrequently, so would the airplane itself. This happens very rarely, perhaps once every four or five years, but it does explain those newspaper reports of: "Jet falls thousands of feet, everyone scared." Sure, everyone was startled, but the airplane probably only dropped a few thousand feet, and that was intentional as the pilot sought to regain his normal airspeed. Remember the captain's admonition to keep your seatbelt fastened even if the seat belt sign is turned off? This is the reason why he made it. It is impossible to predict when CAT will be encountered.

Almost all pilots, when they encounter CAT, will start looking for a smoother altitude but, during the winter season, there may not be any smoother air at any altitude. A few years ago when an intense low pressure area that the meteorologists named "El Nino" dominated the western coastal areas of Central America. The jet streams were pulled further south and to lower altitudes than ever before. For an entire winter season there was no smooth air at any altitude. I know. I tried them all.

All of these things can alter an airplane's ability to stay on schedule, especially when the airplane is working into, or through a large airport complex. Don't be too cross with the airline when things are backed up. The railroad train is not affected by any but the most severe weather conditions, but it doesn't travel more than 500 MPH, either.

✈

CHAPTER 7

MAKING A SAFE MACHINE AND A SAFE SYSTEM

When you start talking about flying safety, every eye turns to the airplane itself. In an earlier chapter we examined the airplane as it exists today. We have also taken a brief look at the air traffic control system and found that it could stand a little tuning up. So let us design a safer airplane...that is if you, Mr. and Mrs. Passenger, want a safer airplane. You may not want it after we are done, for the simplest of reasons: that you would have to pay for it. Oh yes, safety costs money. You and your traveling companions demand safety, but, in the case of air travel, you want to put a price on it. Let's overhaul a 727 and make it the safest airplane in the skies.

A "MODEST" PROPOSAL FOR THE SAFEST AIRPLANE EVER

First, let's rip out the complete interior of the airplane and replace all of those nice, cushy seats with metal seats. Nothing left in there to burn or to create smoke. Even the seat belts are made of a metal mesh. We could serve you dinner in a metal army messkit, but all of those little, loose metal messkits, would definitely be hazardous, flying around the cabin in turbulence. So no messkits and no food. No magazines either, unless they are printed on stainless steel foil. (Nobody said this airplane would be exactly comfortable.)

Now we really have an aluminum tube, with all its not-so-glamorous metal ribs and bits for all the world to see. Since the cabin is sort of a survival cell, the skin is made of high temperature steel, so the fire outside stays outside. Therefore the airplane is going to be a little heavy. It has been a long time since a window has blown out of a pressurized airplane but, just in case...no windows.

We can blanket the walls with Nomex materials, the

same fabric from which racing driver's suits are made. Not very attractive stuff, but at least it will soften the noise of the slipstream as it speeds past the outer skin. The seats, as well, can be upholstered in Nomex. For additional safety, you are required to appear on board, dressed in a stunning Nomex fireproof suit, with a crash helmet.

The entire front half of the ship is a long core of honeycomb material designed to absorb, at a controlled rate, an impact equal to that of meeting a mountain head on. The seats are likewise designed to stand up under crash conditions, and they face backwards. They are equipped with not simple seatbelts of metal mesh, but full body restraints that remain fastened at all times. Breathing air is plumbed to your helmet. In the event of a crash, the entire cabin will be flooded with foam fire protectant, and you will be immobilized until rescue crews can get you out of the wreckage. The crew is seated in the rear of the airplane and no longer has any real contact with the outer world. Video screens provide all the vision needed for ground movement. The flight will be conducted entirely by the auto-pilot and controlled by ground-based computers. The crew merely serves as monitors.

Since this airplane is designed to assure survival, we will have to crash a few in tests. Using dummies or volunteers (one in the same, actually) we can determine the top speed at which everyone would survive the attempt to drill their way through the face of a cliff. That will be the maximum speed at which the airplane can be operated.

There is very little room left for passengers, perhaps only about a dozen, so the price of tickets is rather high and, since the machine is somewhat heavy, it cannot carry much fuel. Flights will be short.

If all of this sounds silly, that is because it is. No one would tolerate such discomfort and expense. But today's airplanes can, and should, be made safer. Bear in mind that anything you do to an airplane that has already been certified as "safe enough" by the government is going to cost the airlines big bucks, and those costs will be reflected in your travel costs.

A MORE REASONABLE PROPOSAL

Let's take a look at some of the changes that really could be made. But before we get to tinkering with the bird itself, there are a few things that need to be done to the system.

1. First are the procedural changes within the air traffic control system. The desire to move more traffic from too few airports is becoming the national goal of the FAA, rather than a single-minded attention to the safety of the system. Rather than experiment with reduced approach spacing for arriving airliners, someone very high up in the FAA hierarchy should flatly say, "No more! We will operate these airways at what we, and the pilots, know to be a safe distance from one another. If the airlines want to move more traffic, they will do it during off-peak hours. The government will concern itself solely with the quality of safe operations and not with the quantity of flights."

2. Every single runway in this nation should be equipped with a precision instrument landing system. Many airports have instrument landing systems allowing the approach to be made in one direction only. Some sort of non-precision approach may, or may not, serve the runway from the other direction. This writer was once forced to approach a short, wet runway with a tailwind. The cloud layer was too low to permit a landing into the wind, as is normal. When one flies such a downwind approach, it is necessary to touch down as soon as possible and begin to slow the beast. There is not the time nor the runway to fool around trying for a "grease job" landing. This I did, and the landing was quite firm, and each passenger let me know of his displeasure as he deplaned. I had to bite my lip because I didn't have the time or the inclination to tell them that the capital city of the state of Florida had one of the most marginal airports in the nation. I had always heard that it is a poor workman who blames his tools. Incidentally, this same airport did build a second runway, complete with a precision landing system. No jet airliner should ever approach a runway not so equipped.

3. No jet airliner should approach a runway that lacks a visual approach slope indicator light system. This is a simple set of high intensity lights, located to the side of the touchdown point that, through a changing pattern of colored lights, informs the approaching pilot if he is too high, too low or right on the proper descent angle. A little rain and a lot of darkness can be especially confusing to pilot who is approaching a "black hole" runway with no vertical guidance. Such a condition should not be tolerated

4. When speaking of collision avoidance, nothing can do the job better than for the crew of at least one airplane to see the other. There is a system that is already installed on many of the world's airliners that makes this a lot easier. The LOGO light.

On these aircraft, a pair of spotlights are installed in the horizontal tail surfaces that illuminate the vertical tail: the rudder. These originally were installed as a promotional device. The airline's symbol, painted on the vertical surface, was lit up like a large, mobile billboard. Easily visible as the airplane taxied around major airports, these large, illuminated surfaces also help other pilots see the aircraft in flight. These lights could be made mandatory on all aircraft, large and small, and their use made a requirement.

On this same subject, one can only wonder at the fate of Korean Airlines flight 007 had the tail of the 747 been identifiable to the Russian fighter pilot who intercepted it. It is entirely possible that there were logo lights installed on the 747, but not turned on. What were the policies regarding the use of the logo light at the time of the loss of 007? What are they today? What if international law had required their use on all flights? Could any fighter pilot, even a Russian defending his country's most sensitive territory, knowingly send a missile into what he had identified as a civilian airliner?

5. The electronics industry should enter into a crash program (maybe a poor choice of words) to develop an onboard Doppler radar system that can display to the pilot, in real time, the potential of a windshear encounter. There is no time for a ground controller to see, evaluate, and issue a lengthy windshear alert. By the time he has done this, the pilot on final approach has already encountered the downdraft.

6. As badly as the controller needs upgraded equipment, the proper place to put the new Collision Avoidance Systems and Windshear Alert Systems is in the cockpit. When a potential problem develops in windshear or collosion, it occurs in a hurry. There is no time for someone to communicate a course of action to the pilot. He is there, in real time, and the controller is elsewhere, perhaps dealing with another airplane. Situations that require fast action demand that the information be given immediately to the one who has to take that action.

One person once insisted to me, 15 years ago, that within the span of my career the controller would actually be "flying" my airplane, through a system called "Data Link." The controller, or his ground-based computers, would literally be controlling the autopilot and throttles, with no consultation with me. My reply to him need not be repeated here.

7. An entirely new method of communications needs to be worked out. There should possibly be a printer in the cockpit or a display that informs the pilot what the controller wants him to do and provides a way for the pilot to respond that he has received the clearance and will comply. The present voice communications procedures are far too cumbersome and time-consuming. They also carry with them one of the greater dangers in the Air Traffic Control system, that of simultaneous transmissions. If two transmitters are keyed at one time, no one hears anything but a loud squeal. At the same instant, both transmitting parties hear only their own voices. Each thinks that his transmission has been received, but neither has been. This happens many times a day. The only time a pilot should touch a transmitter button is if, for whatever the reason, he cannot comply with a clearance as displayed in his cockpit. The FAA is aware of this need and, well, "studies are on-going..."

8. Now, let's move into the cabin area and see what can be done to improve safety there. I believe there is a need for an easily accessible "full head smoke hood" that would provide the occupant of a smoke-filled cabin enough time to evacuate without succumbing to the smoke itself. This idea has been proposed for several years to the FAA, but so far nothing has come of the it and people have died of smoke inhalation in an otherwise survivable accidents. "Studies are on-going..."

Such a device should be simple to manufacture. The upper half of the hood would be a clear plastic bubble, large enough to fit over eyeglasses or very fat heads. The lower half, all the way around, would be a chemically treated gauze-like filtration material and drop all the way to the shoulders, with a simple draw string to seal it around the neck. The plastic would be treated with some sort of anti-fog chemical, so that a person's breath would not obscure his vision. Primitive, yes, and it wouldn't work very long in heavy smoke, but it would work long enough for the person to get out of a smoky cabin. It would be better than nothing.

The cabin of a modern airliner is loaded with materials that, when subjected to the intense heat of a fire, produce great quantities of lethal smoke, so thick and greasy that one good inhalation can reduce a passenger's ability to escape to nil. Fireproof and smokeproof materials can, and should, replace all of this material. When will this be done? "...Studies are under way and changes will be made when appropriate." If you just happen to be in a smoke-filled cabin, the appropriate time was yesterday. The irony is that the smoke hoods actually exist and are advertised in some magazines. However, none are approved by the government. "Such systems are being evaluated..."

9. Along these lines, how about several "emergency smoke evacuation panels" located in the cabin roof that would, when activated, suck any smoke overboard from the ceiling, where the smoke tends to rise anyway. Such a system would need to be engineered into new aircraft and a fairly simple modification would be required for existing machines. A simple "suction blower" would help reduce smoke within the cabin when the airplane is on the ground, enhancing evacuation attempts. During flight, these panels, when opened, would allow the pressurization and the smoke to quickly escape overboard and would require no blowers. Yes, the cabin would depressurize and oxygen masks would be required until the crew could descend to a lower altitude, perhaps four minutes. The rapid evacuation of the residual smoke would allow the crew to more rapidly identify the source of the fire and to extinguish it quickly. Cabin fires are extremely rare, and those that do occur almost always originate in the lavatories. They are almost always caused in the same way. A smoker, unable to get a seat in the smoking section of the airplane, goes into the lavatory for a quick puff or two, then drops his smoldering cigarette in the trash bin. POOF...a paper towel ignites, or at least smokes a lot.

Most aircraft lavatories have automatic fire extinguishers that will put out the fire, once it becomes an actual fire. Until then, it can create a lot of smoke. If you like to assign blame for things like this, you can either blame the smoker for not following the rules (it is against federal law to smoke in an airplane lavatory), or the anti-smoking zealots who

--- ✈

have driven him to "sneak a smoke" where he shouldn't. (Note: As this book is being completed, smoke detectors are being installed in airplane lavatories.)

10. Cabin emergency lighting could be improved with the installation of high intensity, flashing strobe lights. Getting more exotic, an externally-mounted infrared sensor would disable an exit's strobe lights if the presence of a fire were detected outside the exit. The absence of strobe lights would discourage passengers from opening an exit only to find that they were unable to use it, and even worse, allow the fire and smoke into the cabin. They would look for strobes that were flashing and use that exit as their secondary exit. (After numerous reports of the inadequacy of emergency lighting installations, new lighting is being installed where it will do some good. On the floor, light strips are being installed that can lead to exits. These should be much better since smoke can rise and obscure the old, ceiling mounted lights.)

11. The design, construction and deployment of emergency evacuation slides should be re-evaluated. On several recent incidents, emergency operation of doors and exits simply did not work, and automatic deployment of slides and chutes either did not work or caused injuries in their use. Even properly deployed slides can be useless, if the wind is blowing very hard. The slides are simply blown back against the side of the aircraft.

12. No hazardous material of any kind, unless involved in a medical emergency, should be permitted on a passenger flight, yet these materials are carried every day. The FAA and the airlines have devised procedures that are supposed to insure the safety of aircraft and their passengers by requiring complex packaging and markings and by restricting the types of materials that can be transported. The procedure works great as long as everyone plays by the rules. Unfortunately, we don't live in that sort of society, and nothing can stop the clever shipper from sending a glass jar of highly corrosive acid in a package marked, "Christmas Ornaments." Sure, the guy can be fined, after one of his bottles breaks and spills enough acid to eat its way through the skin of the airplane and maybe a few control cables as well. (All the while it is creating highly toxic fumes.)

There are other things that could be done to improve the safety of the air traveler. None of it will be done until you, friend reader, demand it of the airlines and, more importantly, your government. Also, you must be ready to accept the increased cost of safety improvements because you know where the cost of such modifications is going to show up . . . in your ticket price. There never has been, nor will there ever be, a free lunch. As long as you, the bargain hunting passenger, seek only the cheapest ticket prices, nothing will be done. You may not like hearing that, but it is the simple truth.

I've done a whole lot of talking about flying safety and how it could be improved. Sure it can be improved and, ultimately, will be. It will be when the traveling public demands it or when someone dies. The cost of safety improvements should not be even a tiny consideration of a federal agency whose responsibility is air safety.

Remember, the airlines simply cannot make improvements, even in the area of safety, until those changes are approved by the FAA, and the FAA is going to continue to be damned reluctant to approve anything unless they are forced to do so. Even the federal government, when it puts its seal of approval on something, has to face the fact that it can be in court the very next day, defending itself against a huge liability suit. That is why the studies and testing of new safety devices take so long. Tragically, it sometimes takes too long.

But to put this chapter in perspective, air travel is still the safest way to travel around our country and will remain so. You may not like to consider statistics, but the numbers don't lie. The odds of your being involved in an aircraft accident are about equal to those that you will slip down in a bathtub, on a Tuesday, in a motel in Louisville, Kentucky, and break your right elbow. These odds apply to residents of San Francisco who have never even heard of Louisville and, knowing Louisville as I do, are missing something.

➤

CHAPTER 8

DEREGULATION: OPINION

So far, it may appear that this book was designed to reassure the passenger, and it was. I sincerely believe that what I, and all the rest of the airline people of America, are doing is providing safe, comfortable air transportation. I am proud of the job that we have done for the public, and we are going to keep on doing the same.

But to pretend that there are no flaws in the air travel industry, to tell you just the things that I think you want to hear and to smear make-up over the ladies' warts, would be dishonest. Understand something else. I promised you, at the very beginning of this book, that I wouldn't be waving a lot of statistics at you, and I won't. Everyone knows that you can make numbers say pretty much anything that you want them to say.

What I have to say on this subject, the matter of deregulation, is not compiled from a lot of numbers, but are my own feelings on the subject. These are feelings that I get out on the line, in the cockpit, hearing air traffic controllers: the tone of their voices. They are the feelings I get when I pick up an aircraft maintenance log and discover things that should have been fixed but haven't been fixed.

So, these are my own opinions on deregulation and what it has brought.

In 1978, President Jimmy Carter signed the deregulation bill into law. The government was no longer going to have a hand in the air travel industry. New airlines could spring up and challenge the older, established carriers on the basis of price. These "upstart" carriers would offer competition, and lower fares. Sounds great. The American way.

Uncle Elmer and Aunt Bea can travel from Mobile to Los Angeles cheaper than they can on the bus. Well, not quite. None of the new, low cost airlines come into Mobile.

I'm getting ahead of myself. To understand what deregulation has brought to the airline industry, you must first go back to what regulation was.

THE HISTORY OF GOVERNMENT REGULATION

The real origin of what became regulation of the airlines began way back at the beginnings of the Air Mail contracts. The U.S. Post Office would offer air mail routes to competing airlines. Anyone with a few ragged old biplanes could bid on these routes: they were an airline. Since there was virtually no passenger traffic in those days, the company with an air mail contract made money and the rest took their airplanes and went barnstorming. The Post Office guaranteed a certain amount of money, whether any mail was actually carried or not.

Almost all of the established airlines were started this way. They added airplanes as they added mail routes. They added bigger airplanes when passengers started to show up, but the mail was really paying the bills.

The CAA (Civil Aviation Administration) was formed to keep an eye on all of these airplanes that were carrying mail and passengers around the country. When more passengers showed up, it was only natural that the CAA would also write regulations on what kind of airplanes were safe. They also decided to establish what fares could be charged. Still, the route structures that the airlines built were based on their airmail contracts. Since the Post Office would not pay more than one north/south airline to haul the mail, they only approved one. They also only approved one east/west carrier. That was all the mail there was.

After WWII, the airlines foresaw the potential need for large passenger aircraft. Initially they saw hundreds of large airplanes, war surplus, being bought for a song. The skies of America would be blackened with ex-army transports. The aircraft manufacturers wisely pointed out that airplanes built for war are not suited for commercial use. They are built to a different, lower standard of safety. The CAA wisely heeded this counsel and set a higher standard for airplanes intended for the traveling public.

"O.K.," said the airlines, "but we cannot buy these fancy, new airplanes and operate them for what we are making on the mail and the few passsengers we carry."

"O.K.," said the CAA. "We will raise the fare that you

can charge to help you pay for all of this."

"Great," says the airline, "we will order the new airplanes."

And so it went. Whatever happened to raise an airline's operating costs was passed on to the passenger in the way of higher ticket prices. If one airline had a labor problem and had to raise wages, they merely went and asked for a fare increase. They always got it.

Meanwhile, the airplanes were becoming more complex, more expensive to maintain. When an airline had 15 DC-3s, they could afford to buy replacement parts from the factory. But, when they ordered 35 four-engined Constellations, they decided to open their own shops and actually manufacture their own parts. They opened their own engine overhaul facilities.

The most important thing to realize about deregulation is that there is one helluva lot more to running and maintaining an airline than what you see out that terminal window. During the '50s and '60s, the word "service" meant that the airline had to build shops to maintain their aircraft. They had to build great terminals to serve their passengers. Then they had to pay cities and states for the privilage of parking at their own terminals. They had to build large training facilities for their flight crews and ground service crews. They had to...well, you get the picture. Each airline had to do all of this to stay in business. To build an airline in those days of regulation, the airline executive had to risk huge sums of money, stockholders' money, to get started. Then to keep up, the airline had to have all of this property and material. Then one day...

"Let's change the rules," they said. Let's offer air travel to the masses. Great idea. The American way. Anyone can fly any route and charge any fare. We'll put a little competition in the airline industry, an industry that had been built at huge expense under an entirely different set of rules.

Now, any promoter can lease an old airplane, find a crew and start an airline. No shops, no mechanics, no terminal space or gates. Take out a full page ad in *The New York Times*...CHEAP AIR LINE TICKETS...NEW YORK TO MIAMI FOR ONLY $69.00.

To the strapped traveler, who happened to live in either New York or Miami, this was a good deal. He could afford cheap tickets. So what if the airplane was old and dingy, there was no meal service, and those little seats rammed your knees so far back that you could hardly move. What the heck, you were only in those seats for a few hours, and you were flying cheap. Those cheap fares were important to enough people that the new, deregulated airlines got off the ground. Deregulation was as great as sliced bread with only a little mold.

But, there are a few little catches, besides the discomfort.

Part of the regulation package was that the CAB (which is the agency that replaced the CAA) did not just regulate the flights between New York and Miami. They awarded routes so that even the smaller cities received service. Let's investigate a flight on Eastern Airlines, the carrier that has dominated the New York to Miami route for so long.

The marketing people knew that they could fill an airplane from New York to Miami at, say, 9:00 AM. So they file an application for that route.

"O.K.," says the old CAB. "But, there is no service from Hartford, Connecticut, in the morning. If you want to have that 9:00 departure from New York, you must also have a morning departure from Hartford with a stop in New York."

"Our research shows that only fifteen people will want to go from Hartford to either New York or Miami. It will cost more in fuel to fly from Hartford to New York than we could make in fares for so short a flight. Also, we will have to layover a crew in Hartford to originate that early departure: hotel expenses."

"If you want to leave New York at 9:00AM, Hartford is part of the package. Take it or leave it. The people of Hartford must receive service."

"O.K., but we will have to adjust our fares for the Miami trip to make up for the loss on the Hartford trip."

"We will allow a raise in fare of 3%." Eastern had to absorb the loss of the Hartford leg from the profit it made on the New York to Miami trip.

So regulation meant that Hartford, Louisville, and Brownsville, Texas, received jet airline service, and they received it at reasonable cost.

But the new guy on the block, the cheap seat airline doesn't have to fool with the folks from those smaller cities. All they want is the cream off the top, New York to Miami. If a flight didn't pay for itself, plus a profit, they didn't mess with it.

Simple fact: You can fly from Los Angeles to Atlanta cheaper than you can from Atlanta to Chatanooga, Tennessee: 80 miles away.

Fair deal? Not if you happen to live in Chatanooga or a thousand other smaller cities. Those people will pay what it actually costs to run the airplane. That, super saver, is a whole lot more than it used to cost.

HAS DEREGULATION AFFECTED SAFETY?

Sooner or later we are going to have to address the question of safety. Is the deregulated sky as safe as it was under regulation? No, it is not as safe.

The simplest reason is that there are three times as many airplanes in the air now as there were in 1978. That fact alone packs more airplanes into an air traffic system than the system is designed to carry.

Sure, the numbers: the statistics say that the airways are safer today than they were eight years ago. There are approximately 30% more people riding the airlines than there were in 1978 and there are not 30% more fatalities than there were in that year. Therefore, the numbers prove that air travel is safer than it was in 1978, right? Wrong!

What has disappeared is the margin of safety. The cushion that has made air travel the safest form of transportation in history has been reduced to a dangerous level. At least this is the view of many who live within the system every day. What used to be a comfortable cushion has been reduced to the barest minimum.

The FAA, the government body that is responsible for air traffic control, has made its number one priority the accommodation of more and more airplanes. To not accept, to not accommodate, anything that the industry has thrown at it is to admit failure. Anyone can demand entry into the Atlanta airspace, for example, and they must be allowed in. It is a failure on the part of the government if they cannot do so and the government is damned reluctant to admit failure. So, they keep cramming more and more airplanes closer and closer. It is rather like trying to stuff a 180 pound lady into a pair of size 10 designer jeans. You may get her in, and you may even get her zipped up, but there is an unholy strain on her seams. Sooner or later she is going to bend over.

Sooner or later the air traffic system is going to reach the stage that does not permit even the smallest deviation... and someone is going to have to deviate. They are going to have to bend over and, just like our ample lady, there will be fall-out.

Let's take the example of the tragic loss of Delta flight 191 at the Dallas/Ft. Worth airport in 1985. The official cause, or "Probable Cause," is said to be the flight crew's failure to recognize and correct a rapid descent rate, caused by windshear. There is a large, but unofficial, body of opinion that believes that if there was a failure on the part of the crew, it was not a failure to recognize a wind shear. It was a failure to tell a controller that he had vectored them in too close behind an aircraft that flew its final approach 30 to 40 knots slower than the heavy L-1011. The controller tried to rectify the situation by telling the Delta crew to slow. Then he told them to slow some more. Then more still.

He was trying to keep legal separation between two aircraft of widely differing airspeed capabilities. This he did because the Delta crew accommodated him: they "went along with the system." But in doing so, they gave away the cushion of extra airspeed that may, and I repeat, may have gotten them through the windshear. Somewhere, back on that long final approach, the Delta captain could have said, "Look, I am as slow as I intend to let my airplane go. I cannot slow any further." But he didn't. He went along with the system. He cooperated. It must be remembered that the captain's authority in this, or any situation that may infringe on the safety of his flight, is absolute. He bears the ultimate responsibility for his flight and must remain the ultimate authority. But he must rely on others to help him with this responsibility.

The spacing between Delta 191 and the Lear Jet that preceded him was legal. By the book. But it was not as safe as it could have been. There was no extra margin of safety. The seams split.

There are other ways that deregulation has whittled away at what was once a little extra margin of safety. Aircraft maintenance is another.

The new airlines, the cheap-seaters, did not even begin with a maintenance department. They may have had a mechanic, hired off the street, that had the simple tools to change a few light bulbs, but they saved the cost of large inventories of spare parts and shop space. When something broke that grounded an airplane, they called on one of the bigger airlines to provide parts and technical expertise. Naturally, these mechanics serviced their own airlines' airplanes first, so a lot of the upstart airlines' flights were delayed or canceled. That did not bother them, not even a little bit.

The newcomer had sold the tickets on that flight and collected the money. The passenger was committed to fly on that airline since there was no agreement with any other airline. If you bought a ticket on Northeastern airlines, for example, you flew on Northeastern. No other airline would honor a Northeastern ticket. If Northeastern had to delay one of its flights for an extended period, say a day or more, the passengers had the choice of camping in the airport or going down to Eastern Airlines and buying a ticket. Since you cannot waltz up to the gate of a major carrier and obtain super-saver fares, you paid full, undiscounted fares to get home.

To make matters worse, once you did get home, you could not call Northeastern and get your money refunded. Their flight did depart, a day late, but it did operate. You were not there so they felt no obligaton to refund your money. You just paid four times what you had planned to get home. You are boiling mad, and wild horses could not drag you back on a Northeastern flight, no matter what the savings. But your neighbor just scoffs, "Ah, you just had a bad experience. Look at how much you stood to save." There are enough "neighbors" in the nation that are willing to buy a chance on an airplane ride to keep at least a few of the upstarts in business.

MAJOR CARRIERS MUST ALSO MAKE BUDGET CUTBACKS

Back to maintenance. The major carriers had to compete for the market that the upstart was skimming, and they still had to service those smaller communities as well. They had all of those mechanics, shops, storerooms full of expensive spare parts. They had to pay for all of that very expensive ramp and terminal space, the hangers full of tools and the machinists to run them. They had built up a level of service, over a long period of time, that insured a high degree of maintenance capability. Suddenly that did not matter. The only thing that mattered was to get the public to the ticket counter. The price of a ticket was paramount. If you must compete with carriers that do not waste a lot of money on maintaining their airplanes, you must cut costs somewhere. Somewhere that it doesn't show.

In short, you are going to have to squeeze the cost of running a major, established airline down to that of the upstart who doesn't have your costs.

First came cuts in labor costs. Virtually every employee of a major airline has taken deep cuts in salary over the last eight years. A lot of the older airlines still have failed despite these concessions. The employees have increased their productivity. There is a strong sense of "family" within the airline industry. Members of the family would take the cuts, learn to rebudget their lives to save the airline.

Still the costs were too high. Finally, even the major carriers began carving away at the cushion of extra safety that they had always maintained. That cushion was always in excess of the standard required by regulations. Now, if an airplane barely met the requirements of the regulations, that was good enough. If the book said a certain thing was good enough, then good enough was as good as it was going to get.

It has been said that the biggest decline in the standard of air safety has occured with the emergence of the MBA. People who can only see the bottom line on a computer print-out and are willing to accept less and less "cushion," are straining an already ailing industry. The airplanes are being maintained according to the book...and no further. The redundancy is still there: it was designed into the airplane and is required, even by the books.

Yes, the redundancy is there, and it is a damn good thing. It is getting more and more use.

THE MINIMUM EQUIPMENT LIST

Enter the MEL. This stands for Minimum Equipment List and its first cousin, the CI, or Continued Items. On every airplane there is a book that lists certain items, components or systems, that are redundant. They are backup systems or components. The FAA has approved flight even though one of these components may be inoperative. Let us use the generators on the Boeing 727 as an example.

The MEL says that there are three generators installed on the 727, but only two are required for dispatch. Within a certain period of time, the faulty generator must be replaced or repaired. Remember, two generators are sufficient because only one can carry the essential needs of the aircraft. But by flying the airplane with one generator out, you are starting out with a third of your cushion already gone. You never had it. But the book says that it is O.K. to fly without that third generator, and the MBA says that is good enough.

But the captain of the flight is thinking, as he looks at a weather report that includes a lot of thunderstorm activity near his destination, what if? Remember that phrase? What if a second generator fails. Now the only redundancy he would enjoy is the airplane's limited battery capacity. He would have one generator with only the battery to back it up. He may not be able to use his radar with the loss of a second generator.

Here, the captain will earn his pay by saying, "The book may say that it is O.K. to go into a lot of thunderstorms with a generator out, but the captain of this flight says that it is not O.K. Either the generator is repaired or you can teach the book to fly an airplane." That same captain may very well take that airplane up on a clear day: he now has the redundant feature of clear skies and does not need his radar. Though it is legal in either case (the book says nothing about weather) the captain will refuse to fly the airplane into known weather without all of the redundancy that he can get. At least, this is the situation on most of the older airlines. Some of the newer airlines do not regard the captain's decision as the final word. Pressure is applied to accept an airplane that the book says is acceptable. A bottom line is being applied to your safety, at this point.

Having an item appear on the CI list, an item that needs repair but that doesn't need repairing right now, is not a bad thing. An airplane contains lots of things that are not essential to saftey. Clocks, for instance.

The most basic of regulations requires that a clock be installed in any aircraft that is to be operated in instrument conditions (weather). In the spirit of redundancy, all airliners carry two clocks. The minimum equipment notes this: CLOCKS...INSTALLED (2), REQUIRED (1).

This rule goes back to the very beginnings of instrument

flight. In the early days, the clock, with a sweep second hand, was vital to making approaches. Today, they are rarely used for anything but noting the time of day. The captain's clock is usually set to whatever time zone the airplane is operated from, and the first officer's clock is left on Greenwich Mean Time, now known as Universal Coordinated Time. All log entries are made in GMT. Since every crew member has a wristwatch that is probably far more accurate than the "lowest-bidder" clocks installed on the instrument panel and, since the clocks are rarely used for approaches, it wouldn't really hurt anyone's feelings if neither of the clocks were working. But the book requires that at least one of the two be operating, so the airplane cannot be dispatched without it.

Here is a case of something being required that isn't really needed. But most of the systems on the airplane are needed, as is the redundancy that backs them up.

Yes, budget cuts, in the interest of offering low fares, have hurt airplane maintenance. It was apparent to everyone in the industry that this would be inevitable even before deregulation became the law. The new, low cost carriers would force the established airlines to cut drastically in order to be able to compete with low fares. It could never be otherwise.

Now, you have seen the face of deregulation, warts and all. The system still works, but it is strained. It could be made a lot better, but it won't until you, the passenger, place a higher priority on safety than on the cheapest possible ticket prices.

The airplanes are still being maintained, but not to the degree that they once were. They are still safe, but are they as safe as they could be? Does the airline that you choose afford its captains the final authority over whether an airplane is flown, or grounded? Will they respect his opinion, regardless of what the book says is legal?

The margin of safety has been eroded, the cushion does not provide much comfort.

THE DEBATE OVER DEREGULATION

But, deregulation has provided what it was designed to provide. Cheap transportation. There are those who will say that inexpensive air transportation is worth the reduction in safety margins; the cushion was too plump anyway, and the system is safe enough. A lot of the people who make the system work do not believe this. They also do not believe that the cheap seat is going to be available much longer.

Back in the mid seventies, while the debate over deregulaton was raging, airline executives predicted that there would be many failures of older airlines. Newer airlines, with no heavy operating costs, could easily undercut the fares offered by the established carriers. It was further predicted that many of the weaker airlines would fail. Financial experts saw a time when there would be massive mergers of the surviving airlines: big fish eating the smaller fish and becoming even bigger. Now, in late 1986, all of these predictions are coming true. Huge airlines are being formed and competition is being diminished. Soon, only four or five airlines will remain. They will be so large that it will be impossible for any new airlines to come along and challenge them. With no effective competition, where do you suppose that ticket prices will go?

So deregulation may have only been an exercise in stirring a pot that didn't need stirring. The airline industry of the 1970s wasn't broken. It didn't need fixing. It could have used a little help, a Band-Aid or two, but not massive surgery. In the meantime, a lot of jobs were lost. Within a few years, we will be right back where we were before the whole deregulation business started, with one exception.

The margin of safety will be slimmer. There will still be too many airplanes in the skies of America and not enough airports on which they can land.

CHAPTER 9

EXAMINATION: "...With Liberty and Justice for Some"

If you have been able to stay with me this far, you are either interested in the subject matter, or you are a mental masochist and determined to get your money's worth by finishing. If you are one of those types of people whose imagination is vivid, if you are able to immerse yourself into an idea and become part of it, you might want to give this chapter a try.

To participate in this exercise may prove nothing to you, or it may give you some real insight as to the type of mind that the profession of flying attracts. This insight, in turn, could lead you to trust the man in the front end of your airplane. It will give you some hint of the range of his responsibilities. He cannot simply learn and operate the tools of his trade, but one day, he may be called to account for himself to others.

If you are ready, we'll get started.

By the authority vested in me, by me as the writer, I am going to place you in the cockpit and in command of a massive Boeing Stratocruiser, a double-decked airliner powered by four thundering reciprocating engines. The age of the jet has not caught up with you yet. By that same authority, I am bestowing on you more than twenty years of flying experience, both in wartime and in peace. You have logged many thousands of hours in several different types of airliners. You are the captain.

The four-engined airliner is high over the Pacific Ocean, bound from Hawaii to San Francisco. The night air is clear and smooth and the westerly winds at your altitude are helping you along nicely. You have just passed the "point of no return," that point in space where you must continue on to San Francisco because to turn back to Hawaii, flying against those same winds, would take you longer. You are committed.

If you are ready, you can take your seat—the left seat. The seat is leather, fragrant as only leather can be, and you have squirmed your body down into a position that affords you as much comfort as possible. The lights have been turned very low to allow you to develop your night vision. You don't really expect to see anything out there over the black expanse of the sea, except perhaps one other airplane, westbound to the islands you are leaving behind, or perhaps you may see the lightship floating below in the dark. The lightship is a maritime navigational aid that also is a comfort to passing airmen, sliding through another ocean. Before you, on the instrument panel, a maze of friendly faces looks back at you. You need not read the story of pressures, temperatures or headings that they tell in their quivering. A sweep of the eye tells you, from the position of each needle, that all is well in your darkened world

In the little office that you have called your home away from home for a lot of years, there are the noises of your trade. The synchronized throbbing of the four big piston engines almost makes you think of a factory. You hear the whine of a half dozen inverters and the occasional clink of some metal thing touching another and just the slightest suggestion of a vibration, a tremor that does not belong in the general clamor. You glance at your instruments...nothing there. Turning slightly, you look back at the flight engineer's panel; again nothing. Every instrument is indicating normal and you return your attention to the windshield.

There is the lightship, right on the nose. There are steady winds tonight, not shifting around. The navigator has not called you a new heading in the last hour and you are still exactly on course. Maybe you take a moment to reflect that your airplane, as modern as they come, almost new, in fact, is still being navigated by the stars, exactly as the ancient mariners found their way across the vast oceans. Are you all that much different from...there's that damn quiver again, and you gently place your fingertips on the throttle knobs in the hope that the long cables that stretch from the thundering engines to the throttles will tell you a story. No, it's gone again. Maybe you are getting too old for this business. Maybe you are feeling things that are not there. The copilot looks down at your hand as you lift each finger and replace it on the throttles. He will be wondering what his elder is doing. He has felt nothing except the need for coffee.

The lightship disappears beneath the nose, right on time, and the night closes in again. Except for a few dim stars, there will be nothing to see until the coast of California begins to appear in the early morning light. The dark gray jumble of the mountains will thrust up through the morning fog that always lies on the bay during this time of year.

"Why," you silently ask no one in particular, "should I be asked to fly this beast across six and a half hours of open ocean, only to be faced with a tight approach to a fog-shrouded runway. Life should show more fairness to those of us who must fly the late night show."

"It has always been my conviction," you announce out loud, "that, had the good Lord meant for man to witness the sunrise, he would have scheduled it to occur later in the day, say, somewhere around noon."

If anyone in the crew was in the process of formulating a clever reply to this proclamation, that reply is lost in the hard jolt that shoots through the airplane. Instantly all eyes lock on the instruments and the hair rises on the back of every neck. These little round gauges shivering behind their little round glass faces will tell you, must tell you, what is happening. If you can only catch one of them telling a different story from that of its neighbor.

"Captain, the oil temp on number 1..."

Thump!

All see the number one tachometer dip slightly, then swing back toward its proper position...but it never makes it.

Thump...thump, thump...CRACK!

"What in...?" The question is cut short by the sound of the number one engine, racing, howling, unrestrained. The tachometer now tells the story as it snaps over to the stop. The engine is throbbing at well over twice the highest figure on the instrument.

"Damn...!"

"SHUT IT DOWN...SHUT IT DOWN," you yell toward the flight engineer.

As the airplane lurches violently to the left, you shout toward the copilot, "HELP ME FLY THE SON OF..."

WHAM! The shock that rips through the airplane

almost tears your hands from the wheel.

Suddenly it is almost silent in the cockpit, even though the other three engines continue their steady drone. The nose of the stricken machine continues to drag to the left. A bright, orange flash from the left side window, and you twist in your seat in time to watch searing flames vomit past the open cowl flaps and back over the left wing. In the brilliant illumination of the fire you subconsciously receive the image that the number one propellor is gone — the whole damned nosecase of the engine is gone, and the engine itself is hanging down at an unnatural attitude.

"SHOOT THE BOTTLE...SHOOT IT, NOW."

You watch in horror as a white puff of smoke, the fire extinguishing agent, flashes back out of the mangled mass with no effect. The flames continue to blast back.

"TRANSFER...SHOOT IT AGAIN." Again the puff. Again, no effect...wait, the flames are lessening just a bit.

"TURN BACK TOWARD THE LIGHTSHIP, WE MAY HAVE TO DITCH...TURN RIGHT, FOR HEAVEN'S SAKE, TURN RIGHT...DON'T TURN INTO THE DEAD SIDE."

"Skipper, I can't hold altitude," the copilot's voice is quavering.

"Screw the altitude, keep the speed up," you reply, not shouting this time. "We need some power up here. Give me mixture...rich, and props up to 2200."

You try to regain control of your own voice. Unless you can reel in all of the emotions that are on the verge of splintering here in the cockpit, then none of you has a prayer of survival. There must be about three gallons of pure adrenalin coursing through the veins of each man.

You swing around, again looking out of the window, praying to every god in the known universe. "Oh, please, let it be gone. Let the accursed fire be gone, before it burns through the main wingspar, into the fuel tank, turning my crippled airplane into a brief, tumbling meteor plunging into the sea."

The flames are gone. Only a dull, orange glow seeps from within the twisted mess that used to be a 3500 horsepower airplane engine. Even as you watch, the glow pulsates and is gone.

"FIRES OUT," you shout in jubilation, as if all of your troubles have ceased. "What fire?" the flight engineer asks,

"I didn't get a bell...or a light. Why did I shoot both bottles to an engine that gave me no bell or light?" From his position back in a little cubbyhole, with no window, the flight engineer's world consists only of the dimly lit faces of his instruments, and none of them had mentioned a fire. Apparently, the fire warning sensors had been ripped out when the nosecase of the engine tore free.

"All right, let's all settle down. Let's see what damage we have, what we have to work with." It has only been a little over 90 seconds since all hell broke loose, but if there is to be any hope of coming out of this thing, there has to be some organization restored. You, Captain, are going to have to restore order, and assess your losses and your assets. The airplane is shuddering as the slipstream blasts past the deformed junk of the left outboard engine. The altitude is slowly unwinding, the rolling ocean ever closer to the belly of your ship.

"See what kind of altitude you can maintain and keep heading toward the lightship," you speak as calmly as you can to the copilot. He's flying the beastie, so let's get him settled down.

"TURN THAT DAMN LIGHT OUT!" you all shout in unison. The flight attendant has burst through the cockpit door and the cabin lights, now turned up bright, are dazzling.

"WHAT THE HELL'S GOING ON? THE PEOPLE ARE ALL TERRIFIED!" she almost shrieks.

With all the firm calmness you can muster, you turn in your seat. "Come in and shut the door. NOW!"

"Oh God, I'm scared. We felt the explosion and saw the fire. What's happening? I fell down." Then she bursts into sobs. You can't let the passengers see her like this.

"Stay here, and try to be quiet. Get hold of yourself. We are very busy right now. Settle down and I will talk to the people. The worst is over."

That last lie is one you will have to repeat to the passengers, now paralyzed with fright, and unless you can calm them, the fright will soon give way to pure panic. There is no way on earth that you can speak calmly into a microphone, reassuring anyone that all is well, with the memory of those flames still only a few moments old. But it has to be done, or none of them will survive a ditching.

You pick up the cabin mike, fighting to control the

➤

trembling in your hand. Take a deep breath. You better make this short, because your voice will never last through a long speech.

"FOLKS, THIS IS THE CAPTAIN," your voice booms through the cabin, startling the passengers. A few cry out at the sudden voice from nowhere and everywhere.

"I DON'T NEED TO TELL YOU THAT WE HAVE HAD A PROBLEM WITH ONE OF OUR ENGINES. YOU ALREADY KNOW THAT." (You bet your sweet lives, we've had a problem.) "...BUT THE WORST IS OVER NOW. JUST RELAX, AND I'LL TALK TO YOU AGAIN AS SOON AS WE HAVE EVERYTHING UN-DER CONTROL UP HERE." That was a dumb thing to say, you think as you let the microphone drop to the floor. Your hand is trembling too hard to even try to find the little hook for the microphone. The last thing in the world that those people back there want to hear is that things are NOT under control. Oh, well, you did your best. You will get back to them as soon as you can figure out something constructive to say.

"We are holding three thousand, but she is still shaking, and she is trying to roll to the right," the copilot informs you.

Another bell starts ringing in your overloaded brain. "Did he say, to the right? But the dead engine is on the left. How can the airplane be rolling away from the dead engine? But, sure enough, the wheel is being held hard to the left. This can't be.

You flip on the switch marked "Ice Light" and turn, once again, to look out at the lifeless engine. Now the drooping silver cowling reflects the feeble light, a gaping hole in the front where the propellor hub had once been, is now dull black. The lower cowling panel had been torn or burned away. But why should the airplane be rolling to the...Oh, sweet Jesus! The white plume dancing back over the wing answers the question. When the propellor tore loose, it must have whirled, like a giant buzz saw, back over the wing, puncturing a large gash as it went, a large gash in the number one fuel tank. The low-pressure, high-speed slip-stream is literally sucking the life blood out of the tank. Soon, exactly one fourth of the remaining fuel will be sprayed out of the tank, a useless trail of vapor, streaming out behind you. And there is nothing you can do to stop it.

"Crossfeed all three engines from the number four tank," you order. This will not stop the flow from the left tank, but will begin to rebalance the ship. There are several thousand pounds of fuel in the right wing's tank, and very little remaining in the left.

What else can go wrong? How many more little surprises has fate got in store for you this eventful evening?

Remember, dear reader, it is you that is in that lonely left seat, out in the very middle of a very dark, very large and oh so very lonesome Pacific, struggling to keep a badly hurt, 75 ton machine moving at a speed sufficient to maintain at least some distance above the cold, deadly sea. This is what you have agreed to do in return for a pretty handsome salary and the respect that the public has shown you for all these years. It is, friend Captain, time to earn your keep.

The crew has all begun to settle down and you say, "O.K., let's take stock." You all know what you have lost. Over 25% of your power, 25% of your electrical power, 25% of your precious fuel supply, some stability and, perhaps most importantly, time. The additional power is consuming more fuel than normal, and the hanging engine is causing extra drag and buffeting.

"Radio, contact the lightship on emergency frequency. Ask for a sea condition report and see if they can offer anything on sea conditions on toward the coast."

"Engineer," you know the man's name as well as you know your own, you've flown with him for years, but right now you can't think of it. "Start leaning the engines, and let's see what it is going to take to keep this old girl flying."

You want to cut down on the fuel consumption as much as is safely possible. If you have to ditch, you want as much time as possible to prepare the passengers, and yourself.

The flight attendant has calmed herself. You turn and look at her.

"We are going to need you in the cabin as soon as you feel O.K. about going back."

"I'll be all right now," she says in a soft but confident voice, "I'll go back and get the other girls organized. Is there anything special you want me to do?"

"Start on the ditching drill and keep the passengers as busy as possible," you tell her, "and make a show of bringing some coffee up to the cockpit."

Startled, she asks, "Why?"

"I want to establish as much of an atmosphere of normalcy as I can. Remember, keep the passengers busy. Keep them involved."

Only a brief flash of the cabin lights, this time, as she slips quickly past the cockpit door. She will be O.K.

"I've got the sea condition at the lightship," the radio operator pipes, still very nervous.

"Go ahead."

"The sea is calm and smooth with very gentle primary swells and no secondary waves," he reads from his scribbled notes. "The wind is from the southeast at 5 knots. They have had no surface reports for over 18 hours east of here. No ships in the lanes, I guess."

You glance back and see that the engineer has finished leaning the engines and that the copilot is intent on flying a new speed. The buffeting persists, but has softened a bit.

You ask the navigator for a new time enroute to California, at the new, lower speed.

"Already got it, Skipper. If the wind holds, and doesn't slack off, it will take four hours and 20 minutes. If the wind doesn't hold, then there is no way we can make California in less that five hours."

The engineer is already elbow deep in his cruise consumption charts. A damn good man, you think to yourself. He deserves a medal for being able to make any meaningful sense out of his books and charts full of numbers. At least he deserves a good cold beer. You wonder briefly if they have cold beer on a lightship.

"Captain, we've got 4:40 in the tanks at this burn rate, with no, repeat, no reserve. The book does not have a figure for the amount of drag we are carrying. If the gauges are wrong, if the wind quits helping, if anything else falls off this damn bird, we are, Captain, sir, screwed." Then he adds, "all of this is predicated on the winds we had at 6000 feet. We don't know what the winds are here at 3000."

So there it is. Twenty minutes of fuel left if you try for the coast, maybe. There is no reserve fuel, and that twenty minutes will only be there if everything stays exactly as it is. To try to cross the mountains west of San Francisco and fly an approach in dense fog, possibly below minimums, with only twenty minutes of fuel remaining would be lunacy. Maybe the sea is rough closer to the coast. A lot can happen to an ocean in 18 hours, and a thousand miles, plus four hours and 18 minutes, you think, as the sweep second hand begins yet another revolution around the face of your panel clock. No one has ever ditched a Stratocruiser before. Do you really want to take a chance that the sea is smooth and ideal for ditching, if you head for the coast, and don't make it?

"Navigator, can you figure me a time for sunrise over the lightship?"

It suddenly occurs to you that you sure as hell don't want to ditch here or anywhere in the dark.

"Three hours and 30 minutes from now, Skipper."

You smile as you take note of the title the navigator has bestowed on you...Skipper. This title is most often given to commanders of ocean going vessels, and you may become just such a commander in a few short hours. Your command won't last long, only a few minutes at best, then you will lose your ship.

Your mind snaps back to the straining, thundering mass of metal that is, at least for the moment, a crippled airplane. You try to envision a ditching approach and decide that just after dawn would be the best time. As you began your descent to the west, with the sun over your shoulder, you could watch the shadow of your own airplane racing over the smooth sea, seeming to back up to you. Then you could accurately judge your altitude above the granite hard surface.

"Captain, do you want me to fly another pattern around the lightship, or head for California?"

The question is there, and you must make a decision. You want more than anything else in your life, to feel those big tires touch down on a long, solid, concrete runway. But the path to that runway is paved with maybes and unknowns. You look past your sweating copilot out his window and see the lightship, looking like a luxury cruiseliner, lights twinkling, reflected in the calm sea.

Make your decision, Captain Reader, and do it now. There is no one in this whole world can make it for you. You, your crew, and your passengers are out there, beyond any help. Consider your options, your assets and your liabilities. Ponder what you have to work with and what you have lost. Reflect on what you know, and what you don't know. But do it fast, because you are running out of time.

Your 20 minutes of fuel cushion is down to 15 minutes, now.
"Captain...?"

By now, you may have recognized a portion of the plot for the classic motion picture of the mid-fifties, *The High and the Mighty.* Faced with the same set of circumstances, they flew their ailing machine, filled with human dramas, on to San Francisco and, with the help of some rather creative script writing, landed safely with the proverbial teacupful of fuel remaining in their tanks. Shucks, we all knew that John Wayne, who by now had won WWII at least a dozen times and single-handedly brought justice and the American way to the wild West, could do it. Then he would go limping off into the early morning mist, whistling a catchy tune. But the story of his adventure was not solely founded within the fertile imagination of Earnest Gann, the writer.

For Captain Richard Ogg of Pan American World Airways, there were no script-writers to tell him how his night over the Pacific would end. He also felt the same howling throb of an overspeeding engine, the same sickening lurch of his airplane. He was able to control the speed of the engine only by reducing its power to the extent that the #1 engine was pulling only its own weight. Shortly after he regained some control of the #1 engine, the #4 engine began losing power and had to be shut down. With one engine dead, another all but useless and the remaining two engines gulping fuel at a high rate, Captain Ogg had to make his decision high above the night sea.

Captain Ogg decided to remain over the lightship (U.S. Coast Guard weather station *November*) circling away the night hours, planning every detail of a landing that had never been made. During the night, he flew several practice approaches and, suspecting that the airplane would break in half upon touchdown, he relocated all of the passengers as far forward as possible. He prepared his passengers carefully and waited until conditions were as perfect as possible, then he ditched alongside the lightship, whose lifeboats were already launched.

The ditching was a success, a textbook water landing. The airplane did break in half and was lost. Thirty-one

passengers, and the crew, literally walked out of the floating airplane before it sank and stepped off the wing tip into
the waiting lifeboats. Most never even got their feet wet.

On the happy deck of the lightship, the passengers ap-
plauded Capt Ogg, and Pan American called him a hero.
He had decided correctly. Captain Ogg chose to stay with
the lightship because that was where he knew what he had
to work with. To go on to the coast would throw him too
many unknowns, too many things that could go wrong.
Everything would have to go right, and it hadn't been that
kind of night, so far, for Captain Ogg. The one thing he
knew he had was the lightship. He did not know what there
was to the east. Were there other ships? Was the sea smooth
enough for a ditching, at that point? (Only a theoretical
possibility in a Stratocruiser.) If he had to ditch in those
unknown seas, would there be time to do it right? His redundancy was all used up. Would something else fail on the
aircraft and force a hasty landing? He did not know about
these things, and he took what he knew to be the safest
alternative he had. He circled. He saved his passengers.

After a laborious investigation, the Civil Aeronautics
Board issued its findings:

> PROBABLE CAUSE: The board determines that the
> probable cause of this accident was an initial mechanical
> failure which precluded feathering the No. 1 propellor and
> a subsequent mechanical failure which resulted in a com-
> plete loss of power from the No. 4 engine, the effects of
> which necessitated a ditching.

Within the body of the report was a paragraph that
should have exonerated Captain Ogg and his crew in every
eye.

> The board believes that this report would be incomplete
> without a word of praise concerning the handling of this
> emergency by all the personnel involved. The board highly
> commends the crew members for their ability in recognizing
> the malfunctions and taking correct emergency actions con-
> sistent with known procedures. Their calm and efficient
> control of the situation averted what could have been a
> major air disaster.

There were questions asked by a few who had no under-
standing of how lonely that left seat can be. These few
would never possess the fiber to command, to accept

responsibility, and they could never understand those who could command. People like this, however, seem drawn to challange the Captain Oggs in our society.

"Why, Captain, did you not continue to the coast? In fact, you remained over the lightship for a period of time that would have allowed you to make California."

Explainations of the hazards involved, the unknowns, failed to convince these few. They were working with figures and bottom lines, comfortably seated in their offices, taking lunchbreaks and playing golf over the weekends. It is fortunate that Captain Ogg, and not his tormentors, was in command of Pan American flight 6 on the evening of October 16th, 1956.

1985-86:
A PERSPECTIVE

During the year 1985, it seems that every time one would turn on a television set the stern visage of a news anchorman would appear, superimposed on the smoldering wreckage of a stricken airliner. With deep concern etched in his voice, he would relate yet another disaster from the skies.

Newspapers ran half-page, color photographs along with pages of print describing the carnage, the human tragedy, the stunned faces of survivors and the dramatic pictures of those who had not survived.

Then came the days of questions that, at least during the media's attention span, cannot be answered. There are always the experts who suspect a certain thing or another happened. Sometimes they are right in their suspicions, but more often they are wrong and do more to confuse things than they do to help. The media know that this "big story" will only last for a few days and, as they do in other fields of reporting, they want instant answers.

Nine eyewitnesses will give nine different accounts of what they saw and, after months of investigation, it will be proven that what they saw could not possibly have taken place.

The simple fact is that, until the real experts conclude an exhaustive investigation of the accident, NO ONE knows what actually took place, but vast segments of the population THINK that they know, all because of some comment they saw on TV or in the newspapers.

1985 WAS A BAD YEAR FOR AIR SAFETY

We've got to face the fact that 1985 was a bad year for air safety, if for no other reason than the media have told us it was. Statistically, it was just as safe as, if not safer than, previous years. Many, many more people flew those friendly skies than had ever done so in the past. The ratio of airline fatalities, when compared to the number of people flying, was really very good. Still, there were those all-too-frequent pictures on the tube. To the sometime air traveler, whose only exposure to airline flying is what he sees in the media, this can have quite an effect on his or her decision to buy a ticket.

The real answers to all of the questions can only come from the National Transportation Safety Board (NTSB), whose responsibility it is to investigate aircraft accidents. These people are stretched pretty thin this year. Budget cuts have reduced the number of people who can be assigned to investigate an aircraft accident. Several accidents throughout the world have involved American-made airplanes, and the NTSB must send teams to assist the other governments in their inquiries.

Let's take a closer look at the tragic numbers of 1985, but let's put them in perspective.

As of mid-December, 2,040 people lost their lives in aircraft accidents, world-wide. A stunning number, until we begin to break it down.

Of the major U.S. airlines, there were two accidents which took 164 lives.

There is a very real chance that the loss of an Eastern Airlines Boeing 727 near La Paz, Bolivia, will never be fully explained. Several climbing expeditions into the mountains of the crash site have failed to retrieve the critical Cockpit Voice Recorder and Flight Data Recorder. There simply is no evidence to explain how the accident occurred. Every procedure that could have been a factor was reviewed and some were changed even though there was no evidence to suggest that any of these procedures were responsible.

The only other crash involving a major American carrier was the crash of Delta's Flight 191 at the Dallas/Ft. Worth airport in August. Here, though evidence is still being analyzed, windshear seems to be the culprit. What appeared to be a little ol' rainshower off the end of the runway was, in reality, a mature thunderstorm with enough energy to drive an expertly flown, modern airplane into the ground short of the runway. One hundred thirty-five people died and many pilots are having long, hard second thoughts about entering ANY "little ol' rainshower" until technology produces some sort of reliable indicator of that rainshower's real potential.

Two other crashes involved U.S. airlines during 1985.

A Midwest Airlines DC-9 had an engine explode on takeoff and crashed, with 31 on board. Unless debris from the failed engine in some way disabled the airplane, and there is no evidence of that at this point, there are no answers as to why the aircraft crashed.

The last U.S. crash involved a Bar Harbor commuter flight that went down near Auburn, Maine, in which eight people lost their lives. Investigations are still under way in this accident.

Two hundred three lives were lost in U.S. scheduled airline operations in 1985. Any loss of life is too much, but when you apply these numbers to the millions of miles traveled, you are still almost ten times safer in an airliner than you would be in your car. There are some real loonies out on the highways.

There were two crashes of charter airplanes which claimed 328 lives.

A Galaxie Airlines Lockheed Electra, an aging Propjet, developed a vibration shortly after takeoff from Reno, Nevada. The pilot tried to return and land but was unable to do so. Rumors circulated that a propellor had separated from the aircraft, but when the NTSB began their work, this was shown not to be the case. There is a suspicion that a small maintenance door directly in front of the right wing root came open, causing the vibration which the crew mistook for a propellor problem, but no one is certain.

Just a few days before Christmas, an Arrow Airlines DC-8 crashed shortly after takeoff from Gander, Newfoundland, fatally injuring 258. Though rumors, as usual, flourish, investigators on the scene (as this is being written) have not a single clue as to the cause of the crash.

During these investigations, an amazing amount of information can be gleaned from what appears to be worthless junk. The control boost appears to have been functioning normally but the flap actuating drive indicates that flaps were at 25 degrees of travel while the flap lever was at the 30 degree position. A small discrepancy that, when added to all of the other bits of information obtained, will begin to paint a picture of what was right with the airplane, when it crashed, and what went wrong. An engine that is developing full power at impact will show definite differences in damage over one that was only producing partial power, and windshear can be duplicated in simulators to see how many pilots can overcome its effects and save the airplane.

Sherlock Holmes, with all of his clever powers of observation, could never wear the boots of the investogators who must wade through the horror of an airline crash and deduce the reason for the tragedy. But all of this detective work takes time, months in some cases, and the public and the media must learn to be patient until the real, and the whole story unfolds.

These investigators are, at this moment, hard at work assisting foreign governments on at least three other accidents involving American-manufactured aircraft. Two of these accidents bring home a fact of modern life, as did the crash in Dallas. The loss of a very large, wide body airliner is going to involve a larger loss of life than in years past, and for those who are concerned at that high body count (and who isn't?), it is hard to remember that the single crash that took 50 lives, 20 years ago, could now take well over 500.

On June 23rd, an Air India Boeing 747 disappeared off the coast of Ireland with a loss of 329 lives. Just over a month later, a Japan Air Lines Boeing 747 lost a major portion of its vertical tail surface. Amazingly, the pilot managed to keep the virtually uncontrollable airplane aloft for an extended period of time before his luck ran out. Unable to maneuver and surrounded by mountains, he finally hit a peak. Five hundred twenty people perished in the crash.

Eight hundred forty-nine lives were lost in these two accidents alone. Very little information has been derived from the few recovered fragments of the Air India disaster, although it is known that the aircraft disintegrated in flight since the wreckage was strewn over a wide area. Photographs exist that show the Japanese aircraft with most of its vertical tail surface gone. There is little doubt of what happened here. But the real question still remains: why did it happen? Within a few days, the FAA sent out a demand that all 747s be inspected. Most of the airlines that operated this magnificent airplane didn't need to be told; they had already started their own inspection programs. Later, it was found that this particular airplane had been involved in a hard landing incident almost seven years before and that the repair work was suspect, but still there is no evidence that this is related to the accident. This answer, as in the other accidents, will have to wait until all of the detective work is done and the scientists have drawn their conclusions. It serves no one to speculate about the probable cause.

The last accident that involved a U.S.-made aircraft is the destruction of a British Airtours Boeing 737 at Manchester, England. It appears that an engine burst into flames during the takeoff roll and, during the stop and evacuation of the aircraft, 54 people lost their lives. If it is proven that the engine itself caught fire, then it will put to lie a statement that I made in an earlier chapter. This will be the first time that a Pratt and Whitney JT-8D engine has caught fire. This is still not a bad record considering the millions upon millions of air miles that they have flown.

The remainder of the world-wide death toll involved foreign airlines and military aircraft including five crashes of Soviet-made airplanes. Combined, these accidents accounted for 606 dead. The causes of these crashes will most likely never be made known to us.

By now, you are awash in the sheer magnitude of the tragic year of 1985, and are wondering why I should devote an entire chapter to this sort of thing in a book that is written in an attempt to put your mind at ease about air travel. That is exactly what I am trying to do. Bear with me.

WHY THE HORROR OF 1985?

In none of the accidents I have described is there even the remotest thread of commonality. Nothing links one accident to any other. Two accidents are being blamed on the failure of the P&W JT-8D, yet one seems to be a fire and the other an explosive failure. These two engines, installed on two different types of airframes, are also two different models of the engine and operated in different ways. There is no similarity here to tell us that there is any inherent design flaw in the basic engine.

Two aircraft were the same, the Boeing 747. Yet the apparent breakup of each was in a different manner. The Japanese aircraft lost part of its tail, while investigators believe that the Indian airplane suffered a large explosion near the nose section. A terrorist bombing has been rumored,

✈

but is unproven at this date. There is nothing to even suggest that there is any basic defect in the airplane itself.

The story is the same throughout the entire year. The reason that this is important to you, the infrequent and possibly timid traveler, is that it shows no major problem has developed in any part of the complex airline industry. No link in the chain has finally snapped and allowed the system to fall into such tragic disarray. No airplane has finally shown its weakness. No engine or control system has developed a fatal flaw. The Air Traffic Control system may have overstressed itself in one case, but is implicated in no other. Airframe icing may have played a deadly part in one accident, but is not even suspected in any of the others, and unproven still.

Then why? Why, after an almost perfect 1984 safety record, should things unravel and bring the horror of 1985?

I have already mentioned that the people in the airline industry live by natural laws, laws that are not written by mere man and cannot be appealed by him. Logic dictates decisions and everything is explainable in physical terms, tangible terms. There is no magic here, none of the fabled "gremlins" cause airplanes to inexplicably fall from the skies. Not many pilots believe in anything supernatural. Yet everyone in any phase of the industry is searching deeply for anything that would help prevent further occurrences like 1985. That concern is your best assurance that this year's events will never be repeated.

So, what happened? So far about the only thing that the best minds in the business can come up with is coincidence.

If there is some great god of chance, or fate, if there even is such a thing as fate, then that may be the only answer that we will ever have to what happened in 1985. Meanwhile, all of us in the airline industry will be working very hard to see to it that 1986 is not a repeat of this tragic year.

I could have left this chapter out, pretending that 1985 had never occurred, hoping that you wouldn't notice. I have greater faith in you than to believe that you would be content to bury your head in the sand and not notice the year's events. I just wish I, or someone, had some real answers for you. In time the causes of these accidents will be known and made public. For now the best I, or any of the experts, can come up with is that one terribly inadequate word. Coincidence.

You can rest assured that everyone in this business is fairly bristling with increased alertness.

UPDATE: 1986

As the final corrections for this book are being made, it is autumn of 1986. Only one major accident has taken place in the U.S.: the mid-air collision of a small Piper aircraft with a Mexican DC-9 over Cerritos, California. Although no final determination has been reached, the evidence is strong that the Piper had inadvertently entered the restricted airspace around Los Angeles International Airport. This heavily traveled airspace is very complex, and invisible. There are no little balloons with signs hanging from them. "You are entering LAX terminal control area, turn back." The pilot of the Piper, reportedly a very conscientious though relatively inexperienced pilot, was new to the Los Angeles area. Perhaps he was baffled by the complexity of this restricted area. Whatever the reason, it now appears that he was somewhere that he did not belong.

Perhaps a collision avoidance system, something like the ones that have been under study for so long, could have prevented this tragedy. We will never know because there was no such system installed—in either airplane. The FAA announced, a few weeks after the accident, that in the near future, a collision avoidance system will be required on all airliners. A system has finally been approved.

Isn't it funny how quickly these studies can be concluded after a disaster such as that over Cerritos?

Later, all smaller aircraft will be required to carry equipment that will allow the air traffic control system to provide enhanced collision avoidance warning capability.

The skies are crowded, more so than ever before. There is no room for even the simplest, most human, mistake. Everyone who lives within the system knows this. They know that the days—the good old days—of blasting off into the wild blue yonder whenever and wherever one wants, are gone forever.

The purpose of this chapter, dealing as it does with the darker side of air travel, is not meant to frighten anyone. To the contrary, it is to let you know that those of us in the airline business are very much aware of the problems that we all face. With every day that passes, everyone in the industry is working, thinking and planning ways to make it better and, above all, safer. We learn from those who have gone ahead and from those who have fallen. Especially from those who have fallen. There is no macabre aspect to the time we spend investigating airplane accidents. Some do so to assign blame, but the majority of pilots read these reports of calamity to find out what can be learned. What caused the accident? What did the poor fellow do, or what could he have done? Most important, each pilot will look deep within himself and ask, what would I have done? How would I have handled his situation? Would my actions have resulted in a different outcome? Is there anything that I can learn from this unfortunate incident?

You can also believe that he will not lie to himself when he begins to answer these questions. The penalty for this kind of deceit is very high indeed.

CHAPTER 11

SOME ODDS AND AN ENDING

I got the idea for this book a few years ago when my airline was offering a "get acquainted" flight to school kids. Local school teachers could bring about 15 grade-schoolers out and we would board them on regular flights, say from Charlotte, North Carolina, to Greenville, South Carolina. A 12 minute flight to Greenville, a dish of ice cream in the airport restaurant and 12 minutes back would cost each youngster about $15 round trip.

With apologies to the few regular passengers, I would talk the kids through the different phases of the flight while the copilot flew the airplane. I would mention the flaps, with a brief explanation of their purpose, and read off the speeds as we accelerated down the runway. Simple things that I thought might put apprehensive young minds at ease.

As far as the students were concerned, I could have saved my breath. Nobody had ever told them that they were embarking on a great adventure and that a lot of older folks were scared to death of getting on an airplane. Their parents had said they could go, their teacher had brought them to the airport and so it was O.K. Their attention was on the Cokes they were served onboard, and the ice cream.

What surprised me were the comments made by the regulars, people who flew often on business, people who accepted air travel as an everyday occurrence but who still didn't understand, or necessarily like it.

"I have always wondered what those flap things do. Thanks for telling me."

"I was fascinated to hear you call out our speed and feel the airplane accelerate, then hear the wheels go thump when you said they would. There really is someone up there who knows what is happening. That's reassuring."

The young people filed off the airplane, thanked the

flight attendant for the Cokes (those who had been taught simple manners) and the only comment I ever overheard was that some boy's brother had a Mustang that would go faster than we had. (At 425 MPH, that would be known as a very "Baaaaaaad Mustang.")

It was the adult travelers who had a real thirst for what goes on in an airplane. So I sat down and started doing what I have never done before — writing a book. For well over two years I hammered away, rehammered and then hammered again.

I entertained the idea of including a chapter on the deep seated reasons that some people have for true fear of flying. I was out of my element there, so I tossed this chapter.

I recently had a chance to do a little market research on the effectiveness of my efforts. I was deadheading on a flight (riding in the cabin) in uniform, and a very attractive young woman commented to me that she was scared to death of the takeoffs. Because I was in the process of correcting my manuscript, I seized the opportunity (actually I never pass up the chance to chat with a pretty lady) and shoved the mass of paper across the aisle to her.

"Read Chapter 1," I suggested as we taxied toward the runway. "But kind of hurry because we will be taking off soon, and I want you to have read that portion of the chapter by the time we do."

So much for a nice chat; she continued to read throughout the entire flight, only breaking her silence twice. The first time was to ask for my pen to correct a misspelled word (I really needed that) and then again, just before landing, when the landing gear was extended.

"That was the landing gear, wasn't it?"

"Yes," I replied.

She smiled brightly, as if she had passed her test, and went back to reading.

I would like to think that, one day, some passenger will stop by the cockpit and comment that my writing has helped him at least keep his monster in the closet. On that bright day, all of the hours I have spent tapping away, struggling with something of which I was unsure, will have been rewarded.

A few weeks ago, I had occasion to reflect on the way I earn my daily bread. A pleasant young woman had brought a tray of coffee up to the cockpit and my crew and I were relaxing. We had climbed through the gray rains of New York and had leveled off at our cruising altitude of 35,000 feet, almost seven miles above the surface of the earth. In an air-conditioned little enclosure, with clear windows, I could sip my morning coffee in shirtsleeves and look out at my world. The clouds below cleared away near Norfolk, Virginia, and soon I could see the scalloped coastline of North Carolina sweeping out to challenge the turbulent Atlantic. "Stay out there, cold sea," it would seem to say. "Here is solid land, where man lives and dreams and builds."

But man was never happy with the barriers, mountains and seacoasts, and was never content when someone told him that the obstacles could not be breached. Thousands of years ago, common knowledge held that a man could never travel the oceans any further than he could see, that once he reached the limits of shorebound vision, he would fall off the edge of the platter that was the earth, and be eaten by a great turtle. Everyone simply knew that this was true because the teachers and wise men had said so, and who was to call them wrong. Apparently the Phoenicians did, and began trading with far-off lands in frail boats made of reeds. They sailed off into the distance, and one could see them sinking into the sea. But later they came back. The wise men had been wrong.

Out to my left were the sand dunes of Kitty Hawk, North Carolina, where, only 82 years ago, a pair of loony bicycle builders had once again scoffed at an earnestly held conviction. The conviction that man was an earthbound creature and would always remain so.

"If the good Lord had intended man to fly..." You know the rest of the line that fluttered about the soda parlors, the farms and the halls of Congress in the year 1900. What good would it do to go up in the air? Hell, birds were meant to fly and man was meant to plow the good soil. It would never be any different. The two bicycle builders refused to believe this ingrained truth, and rattled over the sand dunes of Kill Devil Hill, not just flying, but able to control their destiny... and mine.

During the few minutes that I watched Kitty Hawk drift past my window, I had gone 80 miles, and finished my coffee. That first flight, on December 17, 1903, had taken 12 seconds and covered 120 feet. The length of my 727 was 133'2", from nose to tail. But far more important, I thought, was the fact that behind me were more than a hundred people who, within less than two hours, would be able to create their temples in the warmth of Miami, instead of the drizzle of New York and, if they desired, could be back in New York by dinner. They needed no further reason to move themselves 1000 miles than to visit a loved one, or seek the sun, to relax. I was happy that, for whatever their reasons, they felt the need to go south. Their need fulfilled mine, to fly.

In 82 years, the need to move about the planet has never diminished. Only 66 years after that first feeble attempt at flight, Neil Armstrong stepped off of his craft onto the dust of the Moon. Only a few years before, many said that he would never do it: "Man was never meant to..." The same old refrain was sung by those whose vision was still on the near horizon, watching ships fall over the edge of what they could see. Yet, on each flight I welcome an old-timer who was born during the years of our first hesitant steps off of those windswept dunes, and who remembers flight as a great adventure. I welcome youngsters who will never know any other life than getting on the plane for Miami, and might remember today as the "good old days of the 727s." Young and old, they are both back there in the cabin, thumbing through magazines or having a hot breakfast, relaxed as people are when they are doing something routine. They are not impressed by the miracle of flight. It is something they take for granted, something that our age entitles them to enjoy.

We crossed the Atlantic shoreline at Wilmington, North Carolina, and now the immense ocean rolled beyond the nose of the airplane. Beneath the surface of that eternal sea, far below, lie the wrecks of over a hundred ships who challenged the barriers, reefs and storms of the Carolina coastline. Just as their masters learned, little by little, how to make each voyage a bit safer, I can call on the misfortunes of others to teach me the same lessons.

I smiled in remembering that, during my 22 years as an airline pilot, I have never been asked to pay one cent extra on my life insurance policy because of my profession.

I decided to have another cup of coffee.

"Thanks, Wilbur. Thanks, Orville. I came along too late to share in your adventure. But all of us who fly continue to share in your dream, and we have just begun."